Wyrdwood: The Story of

Wyrdwood: The Story of Dusty Miller

Wyrdwood
The Story of Dusty Miller

by
Michael Kelly

Wyrdwood: The Story of Dusty Miller

> With grateful thanks to Dusty Miller 13th and Dusty Miller 14th, also to their wives Jen and Claudia, for their hospitality, friendship and assistance in the writing of this book.
>
> Thanks also to Soo Catwoman, without whom this would never have happened, and who contributed many of her own thoughts, memories and observations.
>
> And thanks to The Folks Upstairs for bringing us all together at the right time.

Copyright 2011 by the author of this book Michael Kelly. The book author retains sole copyright to his contributions to this book.

Photographic items and illustrations are copyright The Dusty Millers, used here with permission.

Wyrdwood: The Story of Dusty Miller

CONTENTS

A Meeting With a Remarkable Man..7

The Elfin Forest..19

Dusty Miller 13th..41

Dryads: The Living Forest...59

Crafting the Living Wood..85

Magick Bones and Runescripts...105

The Old Religion..119

Little Known Words From Our Pagan Past.........................149

Looking Ahead...155

Glossary..163

Further Reading...181

Services..184

Wyrdwood: The Story of Dusty Miller

Wyrdwood: The Story of Dusty Miller

INTRODUCTION

A MEETING WITH A REMARKABLE MAN

Our train pulled into a station located in Kent, the garden of England. My friend Soo and I had travelled here on a Monday in late September, 2010. We were here to meet an old friend of hers, a man to whom I was to be introduced for the first time. Although it didn't occur to me on a conscious level till afterwards, it was certainly a significant and auspicious occasion, marked by the fact that not only was it a full, harvest Moon, but it was also the Autumn Equinox; signs of fullness, ripeness and transformation. But this whole meeting would prove to be characterised by such synchronicities before the day was out.

We passed through the station and out to the car park, where a small man with a big smile was waiting for us. He greeted Soo, his old friend, then turned to me and shook my hand, saying, "Hello, I'm Dusty Miller." There is a dignity and a warmth about Dusty Miller. His dress, manners and demeanour are full of quiet grace. Although I don't think I heard him crack a joke, he nonetheless exudes good humour, simply as an expression of who he is. His hair is white and very fine, tied in a wispy topknot, and he has a magnificent white moustache. Dusty displays no airs and graces, he's a very down to earth and quite humble man, but there's something about him that speaks of wisdom earned over long years of duty and service. I felt a little like a hobbit being introduced to Gandalf.

Dusty Miller 13th

Dusty drove us to a spot where we could look over the surrounding countryside. He pointed out where the towns had grown and merged; how they had changed as industries rose and fell; the echoes of history still upon the landscape. Then we were taken to his home, where we could talk in earnest.

Wyrdwood: The Story of Dusty Miller

I mentioned above that this meeting was marked with synchronicities, a real sense of the right people coming together at the right time to make something possible, as if it had all been planned and done for a purpose. I should probably explain some of the circumstances surrounding this meeting before proceeding further.

I had long been a student of all things mysterious and 'occult' and had investigated the subject far and wide. But as the years passed, I had focused increasingly upon home and the mythological and mystery traditions of the British Isles. I had by now written a couple of books with mystical themes and was in a place where I was ready to write something new which would express local folk traditions. This is not a book that I could have written even two years ago, as I was still working out my own ideas at that time.

Coincidentally, it was two years ago that Dusty decided to move back home to Kent after spending several years in the Netherlands. Thus he too was in the right place for this to happen.

About twenty or thirty years ago, when Dusty used to appear at such British get-togethers as the Prediction Festival, Soo Catwoman (the same Soo Catwoman whose image was used – without her ever being asked – to promote the punk music scene in England) used to help him out on his stall. Their friendship thus goes back very many years.

My own friendship with Soo came about basically through tripping over my own feet a couple of times, silly little events that would ordinarily not have happened, but which extraordinarily opened the way. I had ordered a T-shirt from her website and somehow managed to forget to state which size it should be. I then received a lovely email from Soo's daughter Dion asking my size. This little exchange, showing them to be real and warm people, led me to look at the website more closely and this revealed that Dion and her brother Shem had a band named Good Weather Girl. I listened to their songs, bought their album, and loved what they did. But if it hadn't been for that extra exchange when I ordered the T-shirt, if the order had simply gone through without further comment, I probably wouldn't have looked more closely and discovered Good Weather Girl, at least not at that time.

My next little 'mishap' occurred when I booked flights to see Good Weather Girl playing live. I wouldn't have bothered mentioning it and would simply have waited and got on the plane at the appointed time if Soo hadn't posted a blog on Myspace about her kids' band. I replied with a comment to say that I was coming over from my home on the Isle of Man to see them, only to be told that the gig I'd booked for was no longer happening. They then bent over backwards to arrange another gig on that same night in order to accommodate me. So it's small wonder that I've become very fond of them all. However, if all had gone smoothly and the original gig had gone ahead, I would simply have turned up, kept a low profile, and gone home. The friendship we now have would probably not have happened, or would at least have been delayed.

As I got to know Soo, it was a constant surprise to me how many interests and perspectives we appeared to have in common. In particular, when she discovered that I had written a book on the Celtic ogham characters and had a good working knowledge of runes, she mentioned Dusty to me (and me to Dusty) and the opportunity arose to write a book about him and his work.

You may be wondering why I am recounting all of these apparently random details, and what bearing all of this has upon the creation of the book which you now hold in your hands. But take a moment to consider how these three people – Dusty, Soo and myself – were all brought together at exactly the right time and in the right circumstances to allow this project to take place. Because this is a very important thing to realise even so early in the book: Dusty, Soo and I are all of the belief that things happen for a reason and that our feet may

Wyrdwood: The Story of Dusty Miller

be guided by a force – a destiny if you will – that will lead the right people to be in the right place at the right time. The right aspiration and positive outlook will attract to you those people and opportunities that you need in order to accomplish your task. And so it is in this case. Those little 'mishaps' I mentioned that led to my friendship with Soo were not, I now believe, mishaps at all. They were the hand of destiny. The proof is in your hands.

Other weird little synchronicities occurred just before the meeting. Although these were not matters of material importance in themselves, they are all examples of a resonance, the universe signifying that here was where I was supposed to be. For instance, the day before we travelled to Kent, I had been visiting a friend in Middlesex. I explained to him how excited I was to be going to meet this fellow named Dusty Miller about a potentially fascinating book project. My friend replied, "Dusty Miller? I met him about twenty five years ago at one of the Prediction fairs. That's if it's the same man, he wasn't young back then." It was indeed the same man (and we'll touch on Dusty's apparent age in chapter one). This was an extraordinary coincidence, but my friend was able to confirm that Dusty had struck him as the genuine article, someone who believed in what he did and was by no means a charlatan, although there was "something of the jester" about him in the best possible sense.

This was an interesting enough little reality jolt in its own right, but a new synchronicity was primed as my friend and I continued talking about those old days at Prediction festivals. He produced a staff which he had obtained years ago from a man named Bel Bucca who had used to do the same rounds, a skilled craftsman in wood. It was a tall, handsome staff with a figure of Odin's head on top and runes spiralling down its length. At the time he showed it to me, it was an object to marvel at, but I had cause to marvel even more the following day when the three of us were sitting in Dusty's house. There were three carved heads of what appeared to be woodland gods sitting upon a shelf. Soo was admiring them and Dusty said, "Those were done by Bel Bucca." I almost fell off my seat.

Curiously, another such startling coincidence actually made me laugh out loud with its unexpectedness a couple of weeks after I returned home following our meeting (indeed after the first draft of this introduction was completed!) I was chatting with an old friend in Croydon online, who I have been meaning to visit for quite a while. I explained to him, "I was actually in London briefly a couple of weeks ago and had originally planned to pop over to see you. But it didn't work out as I had a meeting arranged in Kent with a guy called Dusty Miller." My friend's reply came back: "Oh, I know Dusty, he's quite a character." It's a strange, interlinked world, to be sure.

So many wyrd links (and I use the word 'wyrd' in its true sense) running through the fabric of reality, all converging on this time and place, this meeting with a remarkable man (to borrow Gurdjieff's phrase, which is wholly appropriate in the present instance). So you can understand how I was feeling – a kind of tingling excitement – when we arrived at Dusty's home and stepped out of the car.

Above the front door of the house, a carved face surrounded by leaves smiled down at us. It was the kind of figure often described as a 'green man', although the colour of this was a kind of ochre. The fact that it represented a nature spirit was perfectly clear. Other such ornaments were displayed inside the house.

By the time we had sat down and got settled, I already knew that I would be writing this book. Everything just felt right. I know a thing or two about runes and when Soo had first mentioned Dusty to me on my previous visit to see her a month earlier, she had shown me some of the items he had given her over the years. These were all interesting, but the one which seized my attention at the time had been a small

Wyrdwood: The Story of Dusty Miller

wand, which had been shaped until it almost resembled a blade, a paper-knife or something like that, and along the flat surface of the 'blade' were written runes in a tiny, perfectly formed row. It seemed to me that these were runes from the Old English rune set (there exist several distinct runic 'alphabets' from different locations and phases of development, each with their own variants). However, there were certain runes that I couldn't recognise. This was absolutely fascinating to me as a student of runes.

The first question I asked Dusty, then, was about his use of runes, a subject which wasn't really covered on his website or in the lecture he gave on a DVD which had been provided for me to watch before the meeting. He produced a folder which contained a large amount of reference material and showed me his rune set, developed by his family over the generations. He stood up and demonstrated how they had discovered the meanings of the runes, which symbol caused which effect and why, and he then told me the story of how his ancestors had obtained knowledge of the runes in the first place. All of these things will be retold in this book in their proper place, but for now it is sufficient to report that his answers went beyond what I had been expecting and these, together with his description of how he activated his runes, proved to me – a fairly proficient user of runes – that he was the real deal and he absolutely knew what he was talking about. (At this point, you see, I was still foolishly under the impression that I already knew just about everything that would be needed to write a book after looking at the website and watching the DVD. But Dusty was to open my eyes – and my mind – wide many times that day, revealing depths I had not anticipated.)

As the day passed, Dusty told tales of his personal life, some of which will be recounted later. At one point, as he was taken by emotion when telling a story from his past, it became very obvious to me that not only was he a very capable

Shaman, he was also a man of honour, who deeply cared about what he did and considered the consequences. This was a very heartwarming and humbling experience, to be faced with such an honest and unassuming man. Too many of the people I have met arrogantly strutting about the fringes of the occult world have been anything but. But Dusty Miller is the genuine article.

Dusty with his wife Jen

I was given the opportunity to examine a selection of the wands he offers for sale. These are uniquely shaped pieces of wood which embody the spirit of the donating tree itself (this remarkable claim will be explained fully in chapter three). I have to confess that one of the items I handled, a healing wand made of oak, caused a definite physical reaction in me as it was held in my hand. I felt very light-headed and experienced a sensation like a tugging at the base of my ribcage. This might have been alarming if I wasn't already familiar with the sensation; it is the same feeling I have felt when in the presence of what I deem to be genuine psychic phenomena. At such times some knowledge or insight springs to mind with great clarity, accompanied by a physical response, although it isn't always clear where the information came from.

Wyrdwood: The Story of Dusty Miller

Over the years I have learned to trust such information and this was yet another instance where I had a gut instinct, accompanied by a 'knowingness' that I was in the right place at the right time. The experience confirmed to me that Dusty's wands do indeed contain a living essence, and this particular one resonated strongly with me.

Not all of the pieces were wands, of course. There were also little discs of elder wood, designed to be worn as a pendant. These remarkable objects function as shields against negative energy, whether the willful malevolence of psychic attack or the simple stresses and anxieties of the workplace. Dusty explained that they generate a kind of mirrored sphere around the wearer, which reflects back any kind of negative influence, but allows the wearer to function perfectly normally within. It is a kind of one way mirror, where you can see out but the negativity can't get in. I'm wearing one of these around my neck as I type this now.

Dusty explained that when he lived in Holland, he had many examples of LiveWood on open display in his home, but since returning to Kent a couple of years ago, he has allowed his house to be simply a home, not a place to entertain buyers or the curious. There are still plenty of examples on the premises, most specifically in his basement, where the wood is prepared and worked, but it no longer dominates the entire house. Dusty creates many of the smaller items, such as the wands, in his own basement, but the larger items such as canes and staves are now worked by his son, Dusty Miller 14th, who has more space available and has been ably taught in the art by his father.

Dusty's house was chosen very deliberately. Dusty doesn't choose a home by the usual process of selecting a nice area with convenient local amenities. His first concern is to study maps and to trace Leylines, the currents of telluric energy that criss-cross the earth and which are marked by ancient monuments at key points. I found this process absolutely fascinating; I'm very keen on the so-called dragon energies, and the way in which they operate both in the world and in the personal psyche.

He explained that his current home lies at the crossover point where three main Leylines meet. Leylines travel at three levels: along the surface; beneath the surface, and at a distance above the surface of the ground. Dusty has placed stones at key positions around the corners of his house to capture the flow of energy and expand its area of influence to encompass the entire area of the building. As we sat around the table talking, the three of us were within an area bordered and defined by the Leylines, awash with their energies.

Dusty explained that the stones he had placed around the house to shape the Ley energies channeled the three levels of current through different parts of the house. The living area in which we sat was a place of fairly calm vibration, whilst the basement workshop beneath, where the LiveWood was stored and prepared, experienced a far higher intensity of energy. But most potent of all, he explained, was the very top level of the house, where he carried out some of his most critical works. With a twinkle in his eye, Dusty called this area his 'eerie eyrie', and suggested that if Soo or I – or anyone else unaccustomed to such a highly charged atmosphere – were to venture up there, we would probably feel very giddy and tired as a consequence.

We talked about many aspects of Dusty's work as the day grew long, also many events from his own remarkable life (though I have to tell you that he is a very modest man, and would never apply the word 'remarkable' to himself; it is, nonetheless, true). The fruits of these discussions will be found in the remaining chapters of this book.

After a meal in the evening, Soo and I boarded our train back to London, and my first meeting with Dusty Miller 13th came to a close. At the evening meal, I had also been privileged to meet his son, Dusty 14th, who is continuing the family name and work.

Dusty 13th (right) with his son Dusty 14th (left)

    It is my fervent hope that I may do Dusty proud and may represent his work in a way that is fascinating and inspirational to others. His work, the magical tools that he creates, has the power to change peoples' lives, to bring out the best in them, to bring their hidden talents and potential to the surface. He will humbly shake his head and insist that he is nothing more than a servant to "the Folks upstairs". But the fact remains that this work could not be done without him.
    The world needs more people like Dusty Miller. Will one of them be you?

Wyrdwood: The Story of Dusty Miller

CHAPTER ONE

THE ELFIN FOREST

In order to understand Dusty Miller and his work, we first need to understand where Dusty Miller comes from and this in itself is a quite extraordinary and fascinating tale.

The people of the British Isles have a long and mixed ancestry. Before the Normans invaded in 1066, adding their contribution to the genetic pool, Britain had already seen numerous settlers and invaders land on her shores. There were Saxons, Danes, Angles and all manner of folk of Germanic descent who had inhabited these isles, seizing lands and establishing small kingdoms in the first millennium AD. There were also a very large number of Celtic people, who had invaded en masse in two or three distinct waves and who had dominated the land before the Anglo-Saxons arrived. The Romans too had invaded and conquered much of Britain for a time and they had left their mark upon both the land and its people. So the British people of today have blood mixed from all of these influences, in greater or lesser proportions according to locality.

But Dusty Miller does not claim descent from any of these sources (though he says that in more recent generations his family has taken a little Celtic blood on board through intermarriage). He traces his ancestry and family history back to the aboriginal folk of Britain, who lived here before even the Celts invaded. And the traditions and magic he uses are those which have come down his family line from those early, pre-Celtic people.

What do we know of pre-Celtic Britain? Not an awful lot, though we do know from the archaeological record that the land was inhabited long before the Celts came. Indeed, some recent findings would suggest that Britain was inhabited before and during the last Ice Age. Many of the ancient monuments which are generally associated with the Celts in popular thought, such as Stonehenge and other megalithic structures, actually predate the Celts by a very long time. The Celts may or may not have made use of them when they found them, but they certainly didn't build them.

Fossil remains have been found in England dating back as early as 500,000 BC and Dusty suggests that these British aboriginal tribes were very similar, if not directly related to, those responsible for the famous Venus of Willendorf figure. Indeed, his affinity for this artistic style has led him to keep a couple of such figures around the house.

He relates that there were three main aboriginal tribes in the south of what is now England before the arrival of the Celts. The land was then entirely covered with forest, so these people were woodsmen, making their homes among the trees. Later academics have postulated that these aboriginal folk must have been 'hunter-gatherers', their little catch-all phrase which they wheel out when they don't actually know how people managed to feed themselves. But as Dusty points out, although there may have been a few things to forage in the forest, there wouldn't have been enough wild game randomly passing by for hunting, certainly not enough to sustain a community. So he asserts that his tribe actually herded pigs. Or at least, they kept and herded the female pigs; the males tended to live apart from the females, only coming by during the mating season. They would care for their pigs, moving from place to place with them, and occasionally they would eat one.

There are very few archaeological records relating to the people of this time. Dusty explained that they never built elaborate tombs or anything. They burned their dead and buried the ashes with a stone over them, so there are no bodies to exhume or grave goods to examine. After all, if the dead had been buried, the pigs would simply have dug them up. As Dusty drily explained to me with that mischievous sense of humour, "Although we ate the pigs, we didn't want them to eat us!"

Dusty standing inside a very ancient hollow Oak

The tribespeople held their pigs in great reverence. They weren't simply a source of food, there was also something very human-like about them. If you look at the eyes of a pig, they are not like the eyes of most other animals; they look like human eyes. The men of the tribe used to grow moustaches, twisting the ends upwards so that they resembled a pig's tusks, to express their kinship with their herd. Dusty himself has a very fine moustache after this fashion, carrying the tradition forward into the modern day.

These aboriginal tribes didn't possess an organised religion in a way that would be recognised by religious people today. But they were very aware of the spiritual dimension. They knew that when they looked at a person, they were not seeing the whole being of that person. All that their eyes could see were the person's body and the actions carried out by that body. They knew from experience that there were whole realms of thought and imagination – the entire inner life of the person – that were invisible to the eye and were not part of the physical existence.

They were also aware that other living things shared this incorporeal aspect and possessed a spiritual side which was invisible but nonetheless real. Their pigs possessed it, but so did the other life form with which their lives were closely intertwined: the trees of the forest (we will return to this subject again in great detail in chapter four).

Because they were able to discern these invisible, spiritual qualities, they also became aware that there existed a hierarchy of spiritual beings who were of a higher order. These are beings that might be termed gods and goddesses, but these aboriginal tribes didn't really classify them, they simply accepted their existence and were open to their promptings, following the guidance of these higher beings. As time passed, Dusty's family line has come to simply refer to them as "the Folks Upstairs". This is a reference to the long-established tradition in European cultures that the masters of the house would live on the upper floors while the servants dwelt below. So these higher spiritual entities which the tribes were aware of, and which passed on instructions and guidance to them, became known as "the Folks Upstairs" and that is how they will be referred to throughout this book.

It might be wondered how Dusty's ancestors were

Wyrdwood: The Story of Dusty Miller

aware of this spiritual dimension of reality. What faculty did these people, living in a forest, possess which could possibly have given them insights into other levels of reality? Especially considering that these insights and perceptions were so acute that they believed they were able to receive intelligible instructions from the Folks Upstairs. The answer lies in the tricameral brain.

The human brain is made up of three main parts. A lot of people today are aware of the distinction between left-brain and right-brain thinking, but may not be quite so aware of the earliest part of the brain which lies at the base of these. But we all possess this tricameral brain, made up of these three parts.

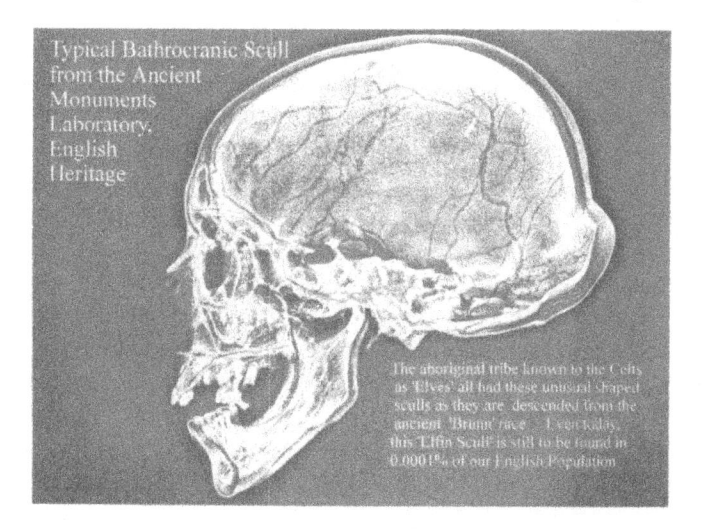

Typical Bathrocranic Scull from the Ancient Monuments Laboratory, English Heritage

The aboriginal tribe known to the Celts as 'Elves' all had these unusual shaped sculls as they are descended from the ancient 'Brunn' race – Even today, this 'Elfin Scull' is still to be found in 0.0001% of our English Population

The left-brain seems to dominate our thinking these days, largely as a result of the way in which we are brought up and educated. The left-brain tends to control the right-hand side of the body and is the centre of rational, logical thought processes. It is the left-brain that indexes and catalogues, that is responsible for language and logic. The left-brain communicates in words and numbers.

The right-brain controls the left-hand side of the body and is much more emotional and intuitive in its function. It is creative and artistic and it tends to think in pictures rather than in words. When you talk to someone, the right-brain would interpret and read their body language while the left-brain was listening to their words.

It is a difficult enough thing for most modern people to get these two sides of their brains working together. Most people seem to see-saw unevenly between the two and this is the cause of so many of the neuroses and imbalances that afflict people today. The left-brain tends to predominate, insisting upon a rational, objective approach to life, regimented and quite inflexible. Then, when the pressure gets too much, the right-brain will take over, often with an emotional outburst and accompanying stress. Wouldn't it be far more effective and rewarding if we allowed both hemispheres to work together? If we used our left-brain's meticulous reasoning and ordered our schedules to achieve the visions and aspirations of our right-brain? If we used the lateral thinking and emotional guidance of our right-brain to decide what projects and works were worthy of the organisational skill of our left-brains? If we can pause for a moment and take time to reflect on what really matters to us as individuals, then it isn't really so hard to do. But the pace of modern living and the demands of modern careers aren't too keen on allowing us to pause for that moment. It's not good to live your life just doing what you're told; remember that.

Now imagine how difficult it must be to introduce a third part of the brain into this delicate balance. It sounds intimidating, doesn't it? Actually, we all use that earlier, more instinctual part of the brain all the time; it is responsible for all of the body's motor functions and automatic responses and it triggers our instinctive reactions to events and stimuli. The problem is, for most of us, it does all of these things below the threshold of conscious awareness as we're too busy being distracted by the tug of war between the right and left hemispheres.

Now Dusty's people managed to use all three parts of their brains at the same time, keeping them in balance. It is this proper balance of mind which opened their awareness to life's spiritual dimension and allowed them to become conscious of their own higher selves (to use the generally accepted term for an individual's spiritual component), as well as the higher selves of the trees among which they lived and the Folks Upstairs who guided them. Dusty's family line has retained this ability to keep the parts of the brain functioning in harmony, thus keeping perception open to higher spiritual promptings.

Dusty's people seem to have retained the knack for this kind of thinking from very ancient times. But we are all human beings, of course, and we all have these three brain elements, just as we all have a higher self and an invisible spiritual part of our being. To support these claims, we find similar ideas put forward in the soul lore of the Celtic and Germanic tribes. To use the Germanic model as an example, when the *hugh* (mind / left-brain), the *myne* (memory / right-brain) and *wode* (ecstatic consciousness / intuition) are working as a harmonious whole, then the individual will be able to contact an altogether higher state of consciousness called the Wode-Self (the higher self), a state of consciousness which abides in the spiritual realm of the gods and can communicate their instructions. Indeed, this Wode-Self is named after Woden, the chieftain of the Germanic gods. The Celts had a very similar model. More on Germanic soul-lore can be found in Edred Thorsson's *Runelore* and my own *Book of Ogham* contains details of the Celtic soul model.

The fact remains, though, that among the Celtic and Germanic tribes, this balancing of the parts of the mind in order to achieve a transcendent state of awareness tended to be a feature of the priestly class alone: the Celtic druids or Germanic vitki. And they achieved it through long training. Whereas it seems to have been a natural talent among Dusty's ancestors, one which has continued down the family line to the present day. As a possible indicator of this, both of the contemporary Dustys, 13th and 14th, are ambidextrous, which may well be indicative of this harmony between the parts of the mind.

It is in part thanks to this tricameral mind (which Dusty labels as "me, myself, and I") that Dusty is able to describe how things were in those far distant centuries. The backbrain is a repository of folk memories and these can be accessed by those whose tripartite brains are in proper balance and who have received the proper Shamanic training to access these deep levels of memory. This knowledge and training has been passed down in Dusty's family from one generation to the next since time immemorial, so he is able to fill in many of the gaps in our knowledge about those prehistoric times which cannot be answered from the fossil record. He is able to access the memories of his ancestors.

Dusty considers himself very honoured to be the descendant of one of these tribes of aboriginal British Wildfolk. The tribes lived peacefully for some 7,000 years before the first waves of aggressive invaders began to arrive just over 5,000 years ago. Dusty is able to shed some light on those pre-invasion times thanks to his inherited memory.

This way of life was threatened, however, when the Celts invaded the British Isles. They had migrated across continental Europe, pushing ever further westwards, and these islands were as far as they could go. Celtic notions of the mystic Otherworld were tied up with the idea of islands in the west, so when they reached Britain, they were determined to settle here and to seize the land for themselves.

What is now Britain had once been part of continental Europe, the northwesternmost part of the great European

Wildwood. But after the Ice Age, the melting of the ice caused the waters to rise and low-lying Atland, which joined Britain to the continent, became submerged, separating the British Isles.

The Celts, of course, were skilled craftsmen and boat builders, and when they looked across the channel and saw these western islands, they believed them to be the Otherworldly 'Isles of the Blessed', and thought they would be blessed by their Gods if they inhabited these isles. So they built their boats and migrated across in large numbers.

Although people tend to speak of the Celts today as if they were a single people, they were actually a number of different tribes, who shared a common history, artistic style and language, but they were certainly not a unified nation.

The Celtic people did all have a lot in common, given their shared cultural background, of course. They all wore their hair down, often in long plaits; they all wore bright colours, and the men all had full beards and prided themselves upon their moustaches. They also wore a lot of jewellery and seem to have been a very vain bunch, the men moreso than the women, taking great pride in their appearance.

All of the Celtic tribes were very aggressive, seeing bravado as a desirable quality. They were forever fighting among themselves, both as tribes and individuals, with the losers ending their lives enslaved to the victors. Even at their feasts, they often fought over who got the 'hero's portion' of meat, the proudest warriors duelling over the right to claim it until all but one were dead.

All of the real work in Celtic society was done by slaves, who comprised about three quarters of the population of each village. This left the warrior class free to boast, fight and drink and generally enjoy themselves.

When these Celtic invaders sailed up the rivers of Britain into the territory of the aboriginal tribes in their boats, they were an awe-inspiring sight. The tribes had never seen boats before, nor had they seen such tall, colourful and jewel-

Wyrdwood: The Story of Dusty Miller

adorned people. Nor had they seen the iron swords that they carried, though they were soon introduced to them as the invaders staked their claim to the land.

Dusty 14th and his wife Claudia with an ancient Yew Tree

Wyrdwood: The Story of Dusty Miller

Within a very short time, half of Dusty's ancestral tribe was dead and the rest had retreated deep into the forests. Fortunately, they already lived among the trees and knew the woodlands well, so they were able to survive, but they had no chance of survival if they had stayed put and tried to fight the Celts. The Celts were skilled metalworkers and had come with swords, whilst Dusty's people had nothing remotely comparable. The tribes had never had to fight among themselves and so they simply weren't equipped to repel an aggressive invader.

So these aboriginal tribesfolk became a kind of forgotten people, who lingered among the deep woods but tended to keep out of the Celts' way. This ensured the continued survival of some of them and it suited the Celts well enough. Although the Celts kept slaves, they viewed these people as little better than animals and not even worthy of being slave material.

There were some quite distinct differences between Dusty's ancestors and the Celts. What's more, many of these physical characteristics have been passed down the generations and are still evident today in Dusty 13th and Dusty 14th.

For a start, these aboriginals were not very tall. And when compared to the Celts, who were very tall by the standards of the time, Dusty's ancestors were positively tiny. As well as the already mentioned tendency to ambidexterity, their thumbs cannot form right angles at the joints, so cannot extend right across the surface of the palm as most people's can. The people of Dusty's tribe also grew no hair upon their chests or under their arms, and their fingernails displayed no 'half moons'.

There were other, more immediate differences in their appearance from that of the Celts. Neither the Celts nor the aboriginal tribes cut their hair. Short hairstyles weren't introduced to Britain till the Roman invasion, bringing such inventions as razors and scissors. But the Celts wore their hair and often their moustaches in carefully arranged braids. They had also discovered the use of soap and prided themselves on cleanliness. The men of Dusty's tribe, however, waxed and shaped their moustaches like their pigs' tusks, as previously explained. They gathered their hair above their heads and tied it up in a ball or topknot so that it wouldn't become entangled when travelling through the forest. They also knew nothing of soap. Although they washed themselves by splashing with water, they fell far short of the Celtic standards of cleanliness.

Because of their comparatively short stature, the Celts called these tribespeople "the little people". Because they were comparatively dirty, the Celts named them "the filthy folk", or "the fairy folk". Because they lived among the trees, they were given the name Elf (or Elfin as a plural). Can you see where this is going? Many of the fairy stories that have come down to us through the old Celtic story tellers are actually stories of their dealings and encounters with Dusty's ancestors, the aboriginal Elfin folk of Britain.

We should spend a little time exploring this idea, looking at how the characteristics of these Elfin tribesmen have influenced fairy lore down through the ages. We can also look at a little supporting evidence from other sources and then examine the implications this has for the spiritual heritage of the British Isles.

The relative height of the Elfin folk gave rise to the impression of fairies and elves being small beings. Dusty himself is quite short, though he claims to be a giant among his people when compared to his grandfather. If Dusty only comes up to a tall man's chest level, his grandfather only came up to Dusty's chest level. But Dusty 13th and 14th have inherited a little Celtic blood, so are slightly taller than the Elfin average.

Of course, although they were a short people, the Elfin still fell within the general human height range: they were at the lower end of the scale, whilst the Celts and Germanics were at the upper end, but they were certainly not a tribe of Tom

Wyrdwood: The Story of Dusty Miller

Thumbs. It wasn't until Victorian times that the modern popular impression of fairy folk as tiny people no bigger than five or six inches became established. When the Victorian storytellers – who, let's not forget, did have a taste for the twee – heard elves and fairies described as "little people", they took the description far too literally and adorned their storybooks with pictures of tiny folk the size of little flowers, small enough to live inside toadstools and so forth. Those images have been carried forward into modern times, but they are based upon a misinterpretation. The Elfin people were little, but only in relation to the Celtic invaders.

Another common image which has come down through the ages is that of the small fairy or gnome wearing a pointed hat. Dusty explains that the Elfin tribespeople did indeed wear pointed hats, for very practical purposes. Since they did not cut their hair, but tied it on top of their heads, it was necessary for their hats to be basically conical in shape in order to cover and accommodate their hair. A small cone, tied firmly in place beneath the chin, was also the best shape for pushing through tangled woodlands without getting caught on branches (the purpose of the hat being, of course, to prevent their hair from getting caught up or snagged on twigs or branches). For this same reason, the hat would not be a particularly tall cone, as this would defeat the very object, making it more likely to snag. But to the Celts, they appeared to be little men with pointed hats and that is the image that has come down to us.

Another common image of gnomes and leprechauns shows them with a beard which lies underneath their chin, whilst the chin itself and surrounding area is bare. Dusty explains this by the lack or razors at the time the Celts invaded Britain and encountered his ancestors. Neither the Celts nor the Elfin shaved, as razors – like scissors – didn't make an appearance in the British Isles until the time of the Roman conquest. The Celts would often intricately braid their moustaches and beards, as they did with their hair. We have

Wyrdwood: The Story of Dusty Miller

already learned that the Elfin used their moustaches to emulate tusks, but they also plucked the hairs off their chins. It is quite easy – though admittedly somewhat painful – to pluck a chin hair out by its roots, as these roots aren't very deep and the skin in that area is quite taut. (Dusty proudly exclaims that his ancestors were tough men!) But it is quite impossible to pluck hairs out of the neck in like manner. The skin there is too yielding and pliable; it just won't work. So the Elfin men tended to have beards which ran down underneath their chins, while the face itself was unbearded. If you examine a few pictures of gnomes and similar bearded fairy folk in storybooks, you'll find that most of them are drawn in this way.

You will also find that most of the illustrations of male fairies in storybooks depict them as little old men, with white beards. The origins of this image also go back to the early Celtic encounters with the Elfin and are founded upon two facts. The first thing to be noted is that the Elfin folk tend to go grey quite early in life. Dusty explains that he himself was grey-haired by the time he was forty. I have to confess to having some personal experience of how this affects other people's impressions, as I too went grey very early. By the time I was in my thirties, my hair was silver. This has a very curious effect upon the way in which others perceive your apparent age. When you are young, you look older than you actually are, but as you get older, you tend to look the same as you ever did, your appearance doesn't change very much. But the other people around you are visibly aging, apparently at a much faster rate than you are. And this is what happened with the Celts. They saw young Elfin men and assumed that they must be born old, since they were grey-haired. What was more, they seemed to remain the same age. This was exacerbated by the fact that the Celts tended to live to approximately fifty five years in those days, whereas the Elfin had a lifespan closer to eighty five years. By the time a Celt started displaying grey hair, he was considered positively ancient in the reckoning of his tribe and assumed that he'd shortly be dead of old age. So it wasn't uncommon for a young Celt to see an apparently old Elfin man, who would look exactly the same age and still seem hale and hearty when the Celt was in his final days. So the impression was received that the Elfin were born old and then remained old through lifespans which extended longer than ordinary (Celtic) mortals. Imagine how strange and unnerving a phenomenon this must have seemed.

This genetic trait has been handed down through the generations. Dusty showed several photographs of himself taken over the decades. He is now in his seventies, but he looks exactly the same today as he did in pictures which date back twenty or thirty years. Actually, he jokingly states that this is not entirely true as he wore different glasses back then, but in terms of his own physical appearance the comparison stands.

The other noteworthy fact that the Celts observed about the Elfin tribespeople was their use of magick and their ability to craft magical artifacts such as wands. Magick remains a staple ingredient of all fairy tales and is one of the primary features of all fairy lore. We will be learning a lot about proper Elfin magick as we continue, but for now we can see that it was remarkable and pervasive enough for the Celts to draw particular attention to it, and it was different enough from the magick of the Celts' own druids for them to be wary indeed of it. Fairy stories tend to portray fairy magick as something wild, elemental and unpredictable, which is precisely how the Celts viewed the Elfin people themselves. And you know what? Elfin magick **is** different, it contains a very important factor which is not directly present in most other magical traditions and we will be examining this closely in chapter three.

I have already mentioned that there were three tribes of people then dwelling in the south-eastern corner of England,

Wyrdwood: The Story of Dusty Miller

one of which were Dusty's ancestors, the Elves. The tribe from which Dusty is descended is named the 'Saelig Silvadobbs' (the word 'saelig' meaning 'blessed') and he continues in his role as hereditary Shaman of that tribe.

The three tribes were all very different, with notable physical dictinctions between them, and none of them would ever have entertained the notion of any sort of marriage or interbreeding between the tribes. People never migrated from one tribe to another. Nevertheless, they were all psychically aware enough to know the importance of walking in balance with nature and keeping peace with each other, being always ready to celebrate and trade together whenever they met up. They also all shared a similar Creation myth, referring to the 'Gods before the Gods', who have become known and referred to as "the Folks Upstairs". They also shared a common language, a form of the early Indo-European root language.

These early tribes were all herders and there was plenty of room in the WildWood for all, so acts of aggression were unknown. All of the tribes were nomadic, ranging over large areas as they sought food for their herds. The beasts which they herded became that tribe's totem animal and was considered out of bounds to the other two tribes.

The tallest of the three tribes became known as "the Horned Ones". They were big and brawny, with an average height of slightly over six feet and a 'big boned' physique. Their faces were large and fleshy, with comparatively low foreheads and big, bushy eyebrows. Their large size and heavy brows tended to give them a somewhat intimidating appearance.

The Horned Ones' totem animal was the Kine, a large red-haired animal with big horns which was the woodland ancestor of our modern cows. Just as the Elves used to wax their moustaches in imitation of their pigs' tusks, so the Horned Ones waxed their bushy eyebrows into impressive horns in imitation of their cattle (it was this which earned them their name among the other tribes).

The Elfin tribe always found the Horned Ones to be very pleasant and friendly when their paths crossed and they were very impressed with their strength. But they did notice that the Horned Ones didn't seem to be quite so psychic as the Elves. The Elves were able to trace Leylines and locate sacred power spots where the Ley energies crossed and accumulated merely by the feel of a place, and they never had any trouble finding the spot again afterwards. The Horned Ones had to take much greater pains and effort to locate a sacred power site, however, and once they had discovered one, they would place a permanent marker at the place so that they could find it again easily in future.

The Elves, with their heightened psychic perceptions, found this behaviour to be a little eccentric, but it has to be said that the stones have stood the test of time and can be found all over the British Isles, marking the position of sacred sites.

Dusty Miller 14th at Stonehenge

Wyrdwood: The Story of Dusty Miller

These stone markers vary considerably. Some are huge, complex structures, such as Stonehenge. Others are wide circles, such as the Rollright Stones. Still others are single monoliths, standing alone. The simplest are horizontal Ley markers. But they all serve the purpose of marking a place of power, and in some of the more sophisticated instances harnessing and storing that power.

There is still a lot of mystery about the megaliths. The Elves never witnessed the Horned Ones erecting them, nor did they know where they got the stones from or how they transported and set them up. Modern scientists don't seem to be able to answer this question satisfactorily either. Perhaps this isn't such a bad thing. Part of the allure of the standing stones is their air of mystery and this is a suitable memorial to their makers.

The Celts were a bit frightened of the Horned Ones due to their size and strength. They were as tall and broad as the Celtic warriors themselves, who were of an exceptional stature by the standards of the time. So they called them an insulting word in their tongue whose meaning was something like 'Big Bastards'. That name has come down to us as 'Goblins'. Larger Horned Ones, or leaders among them, were named Hob-Goblins and were considered especially scary by the Celts. The Celts used them, along with the other aboriginal tribesfolk, as bogeymen to scare their children into behaving themselves, and they have been doing so ever since.

Later, in the Middle Ages, when they were outlawed along with the other tribesfolk, they were termed 'Boggarts' and 'Ogres', and had to keep their heads down and stature concealed whenever they went about. They were cast as villains in fairy stories, there to be outwitted by the Celtic hero of the tale. This image was probably not helped by the fact that they often presented themselves as being rather slow-witted as a defence mechanism, to prevent people feeling threatened by them. This gave quite the wrong impression, of course, as they were really

Wyrdwood: The Story of Dusty Miller

the salt of the earth, similar to Obelix in the Asterix comics, Roald Dahl's BFG (Big Friendly Giant), or even Shrek.

The other aboriginal tribe who lived in the same area of Britain as the Elves were small, like the Elves were, averaging about five feet in height (approximately 1.5 metres). In the area where the Elves dwelt, these folk lived close to the rivers and took the Beaver as their totem animal, but in other areas they preferred the sea and revered the Sea Otter.

Living so close to the waters, they were naturally great swimmers and had a layer of fat under the skin that kept them warm in the cold water. They were skilled fishermen, with fish forming a staple part of their diet.

They had dark, shaggy hair and had so much body hair that when the Celts came they believed them to be animals instead of human. You can still see their traces today passed down in the genetic pool, whenever you see people on the beach near the water, sunning their hairy backs.

These people tended to have a single, thick, one piece eyebrow that stretched from temple to temple, and their beards began just beneath their eye level, so they looked very wild in appearance. They wore no shoes and the hair on their legs extended down to cover their upper feet. Some people today still display this characteristic, with a lot of hair on the backs of their hands and feet.

Because of their hirsute appearance, the Elves used to simply call this tribe the 'Furry Folk'. But when the Celts arrived in Britain, they named them 'Gnomes', since they lived in underground homes, like the beavers who were their totem animals. Much more recently, J.R.R. Tolkien, who also possessed a deep ancestral memory, has made the people of this tribe famous as 'Hobbits'. They have been given many names down through the centuries due to their appearance and dwelling habits, such as 'Woodwose', 'Wooser', 'Ooser', and 'Wild Man of the Woods'.

The Furry Folk were a very successful tribe in the

respect that although they no longer exist as a distinct people, there are very many people in Britain today who show evidence of having inherited some of their genes. Just take a look around you.

It is a noteworthy fact that there are still some other tales that have come down to us through the Celtic settlers in these islands which shed some light of remembrance upon Dusty's people, the Elves. We are all familiar with the fairy tales which are found in childhood picture books, but they were not always this way, and they were not always twee. There are the legends of small races of people who lived deep in the hills and woods, and these are legends which talk of real, physical beings, not of phantoms. We also see references in those tales which were written in the Middle Ages but which refer back to events which occurred four or five centuries earlier, during the Dark Ages. The Arthurian tales are a good example. Here too we read of a race of people who were smaller than the Celts, often referred to as 'dwarfs' by the later authors such as Mallory or Geoffrey of Monmouth. But this is further evidence of the survival of a small group of smaller, indigenous people, who were known to the Celts but were not properly considered a part of their society in these times. We see some of these folk memories recalled or hinted at in later supernatural fiction of Celtic origin, such as Arthur Machen's *The White People*.

Of course, the Celts already possessed a sophisticated idea of the Otherworld and its inhabitants before they ever came to these shores and encountered Dusty's ancestors. So the Celtic encounter with the Elfin and the conquest of their lands does not "explain away" the supernatural world. But when the Celts met these "little people", these "filthy folk", who were strange, long-lived, wild men who lived in the woods and who were undoubtedly skilled in the use of magick, it is not surprising that they assumed them to have supernatural origins. And it is equally unsurprising that such encounters shaped their perception and visualisation of those Otherworldly realms from that day to this.

The invisible, spiritual levels of reality that lie beyond this one are not as fixed and rigid as the physical world. They are seen through the eyes of the mind, not through the physical eyes, and they shape themselves in a way that our minds will understand. Their occupants present themselves to us in a way that our minds will recognise. So these early perceptions of the Elfin aboriginals of Britain have shaped the way all of us reading this now perceive the world of spirit. Not just the Elf-folk themselves, such as Dusty and his kin. Not just those descended from the Celts, or the later Saxons and Normans who heard the Celtic tales. But everyone who has ever opened a book of fairy stories, or watched a Walt Disney cartoon. That Elf magick has shaped us and the way we see the world, so perhaps it is high time that we gave the real substance of that Elf magick some serious attention and respect.

Wyrdwood: The Story of Dusty Miller

Wyrdwood: The Story of Dusty Miller

CHAPTER TWO

DUSTY MILLER 13th

Let's bring things back up to date and consider Dusty Miller 13th, the man I first met in the encounter described in the introduction, who now carries forward the legacy of the Elfin magick and close relationship with trees, along with his son Dusty Miller 14th.

Dusty 13th and Dusty 14th

Perhaps we should look at the origins of his name first, the name given to the Shamen of the Saelig Silvadobbs. The name Dusty is comprised of two parts: 'Du' means a sow, a female pig, specifically the matriarch who leads a herd of pigs; a 'sty' is the pigs' shelter or dwelling place (this is a word which is still in common use today). The two together make 'Du-sty', the title given to the person who looked after the tribe's pigs,

Wyrdwood: The Story of Dusty Miller

most specifically the matriarch sow, and who came to function as the tribal Shaman. The surname Miller was assumed by Dusty's family much more recently, when the surviving tribesfolk were obliged to take on surnames. Dusty is the thirteenth generation Shaman since the Miller surname was adopted. His son is the fourteenth.

Dusty was born in 1935, which makes him seventy five years old at the time of writing, though he looks no different now to how he did twenty or thirty years ago, a feature of that Elfin aging that we discovered in the previous chapter. He was born to be extraordinary, marked from boyhood for a magical mission. Not only did he inherit the Elf blood from his father, Dusty Miller 12th, but also his mother was a witch, belonging to a coven that operated in the south-east of England at that time.

To be a witch in those days was not a matter of open choice as it is today. Officially, Britain still retained anti-witchcraft laws, so a certain discretion was required, and witches tended to be born rather than made; a person born into a witch family would be initiated into the craft at the appropriate age. All of this would begin to change in the 1950s, of course, when the anti-witchcraft laws were repealed and Gerald Gardner openly declared himself a witch and began widely publicising his version of witchcraft, opening a Museum of Witchcraft at the Witch's Mill on the Isle of Man, and writing books. Covens then began springing up across Britain and America at an ever increasing rate. Gardner was in fact initiated by members of the same coven to which Dusty's mother belonged.

It is an interesting fact that although the marriage of Dusty's parents made him the inheritor of two magical currents, the union was not looked upon favourably by everybody. The reasons why are quite intriguing. Dusty's mother was related to the Firth family and her aunt was Violet Firth, who is better known as the occultist and author Dion Fortune. Dion Fortune was a noted member of the Hermetic Order of the Golden

Wyrdwood: The Story of Dusty Miller

Dawn, a quasi-Masonic magical order that flourished for a few years in Victorian England. As such, she was a practitioner of complex Qabalistic ritual magic, very formal and regulated. This made her look down upon the Elfin folk magic practised by Dusty Miller 12th, as dealings with Elemental beings and the spirits of nature were deemed lowly and a bit distasteful by the somewhat snooty High Magicians of the Golden Dawn.

None of this is to cast aspersions upon Dion Fortune, of course, whose books and insights have been – and continue to be – of great value to a large number of people. It is simply to remark upon the class divides that were present in England at that time. The ceremonial magicians of the Golden Dawn, whose complex and erudite rituals were derived from rare manuscripts, difficult to access without knowing the right people, naturaly tended to be drawn from the upper, wealthier echelons of society. Dusty's family were, by their own choice, basically outlaws, operating beneath the radar of 'polite society'.

Dusty Miller 13th

Wyrdwood: The Story of Dusty Miller

Since 1951, with the repeal of the last of the anti-witchcraft laws, and the decision of the Elves to operate in the open in consequence, we are today in the fortunate position of being able to compare and judge all approaches to the magickal world on their own merits, and may enjoy the wisdom of both Dion Fortune and Dusty Miller, which is a much happier state of affairs.

When Dusty told me of this attitude of ceremonial magicians looking down their noses at witches, I remarked that it reminded me of Sir Terry Pratchett's wonderful series of 'Discworld' novels and the differences between wizards and witches, their outlooks and practices, detailed in these books. Dusty is very familiar with 'Discworld' and agreed with me, remarking that the stories featuring Tiffany Aching and the tale of her increasing understanding of what it means to be a witch, are one of the best treatments of the subject ever told. (The Tiffany Aching books are *The Wee Free Men*, *A Hat Full of Sky*, *Wintersmith* and *I Shall Wear Midnight*. They are very highly recommended.) "You see," explained Dusty, "being a witch is all about being in the right place and being able to help people." Whilst we were discussing Terry Pratchett, Dusty also revealed to me that he had been the inspiration for the Hogfather (in the novel of the same name). The penny dropped instantly and will be immediately comprehensible to anyone who has read *Hogfather* or watched the excellent adaptation by Sky Television: the white hair, the pigs and the moustache curling into tusks. But more than that: the jollity, the mythic and timeless quality and the genuine desire to better peoples' lives.

Dusty was nine years old when he was initiated. As his father explained to him at the time, it was traditional to be initiated into the Elfin ways at the ago of ten, but Dusty 13th experienced his induction a year early, because of the pressing circumstances of the Second World War. He was simultaneously initiated as a witch, thus inheriting the magic of both his parents.

At this time, Dusty was boarding at a school near the south coast. The surrounding woods were filled with soldiers, as the army was massing at the coast in preparation for the D-Day landings. The boys spent time talking with the soldiers who were stationed around the school and got to know them.

Then one night Dusty was collected from the school and taken to a hill in the woods, away from prying eyes. He didn't really know what was going on at the time or why everyone was there, but a large number of the witches of England were gathered in that place. They spent the night circling around and around and around that hill. Finally, when all was done, Dusty was returned to his school.

The next day, all of the soldiers were gone. Dusty learned that the Allies had been waiting for a "window in the weather" for the D-Day landings to take place, allowing the planes to provide air support for the landing craft and the troops arriving on the beaches of France. The large scale ritual he had participated in the previous night had generated a cone of power sufficient to open up this window in the weather and turn the tide of the war. And now the landings had taken place and the soldiers who had been assembled on the south coast of England were gone, fighting in a foreign land.

Dusty later learned that two thirds of these men, who he had spoken with and befriended in the woods around the school, had been killed in the fighting. He was only nine years old at the time this happened and had been taken along to participate in this ritual. But it is so typical of the man that as he told me this story he was overcome with emotion. He said, "I have often wondered whether we did the right thing." There is no way that Dusty could be held responsible for the events of that time, but it is his nature to consider the consequences of his actions. Anyone who enters the magical world with such a moral compass is not going to go far wrong. Dusty proved his caring credentials at a very early age. It is not enough to have

Wyrdwood: The Story of Dusty Miller

the ability to do something; you also need to have the understanding to decide whether it is right to do that something.

As the years passed, Dusty was taught in the ways of Elfin magic by his father and grandfather, Dusty Miller 12th and 11th respectively. He still possesses his grandfather's wand now and affirms that it works so well that he would never part with it. When pushed for the value he places upon it, he sat back in his chair, thought for a long moment, then said, "Hmm, well a starting offer would have to be in the region of a large, four-bedroomed house, with a lot of land."

Dusty Miller 12th, Dusty 13th's Father

It was while he was still young that Dusty learned how to time travel. Not physically, of course, but he learned the means to send his mind back through time and watch ancient events unfold as an observer. This technique, coupled with the ancestral memory he bears as hereditary Shaman of his tribe, has helped him to fill in a lot of the details about Britain's lost and distant past.

When asked about the technique of projecting consciousness back through time like this, Dusty chuckles and says, "Well, Terry Pratchett tells you the secret quite clearly in his book *Johnny and the Bomb*. It's not one of the Discworld

Wyrdwood: The Story of Dusty Miller

series of novels, it's a different story. But if you read between the lines, the secret of time travel is explained in that book quite plainly." People tend not to notice such things when they're revealed in works of fiction, of course, assuming that it's 'not real'. Well, now you know better and you know where you can go to find the secret of time travel. I'll leave you with that reference to look up for yourselves, so that you can learn the wonders that can be told in stories, and remember that sense of wonder and discovery for the future. It will serve you well.

Later, Dusty was to spend time serving in the Armed Forces himself. He wryly commented, "You know, one of the things they always tell you is don't volunteer for anything." Dusty, of course, did volunteer. To be precise, he volunteered to try out a new design of boot, to discover if it would be suitable for prolonged marching. Of course, there was more to it than that.

The volunteers were shown into a chamber, where they were met by the sinister and rather disconcerting figure of a doctor wearing a gas mask. "Now then," he explained, "we're going to test the effects of exposure to nerve gas upon you. Don't worry, it won't be a lethal dose." Which was fine reassurance coming from the guy wearing the gas mask, of course.

They sat in this chamber for quite some time and were finally led out, thankfully all still alive. But their eyes had shrunk right down to pinprick sized dots, the coloured part of the eyes having disappeared completely. Their vision was severely impaired, as if they were wearing blinkers, able to see only directly ahead and then only very vaguely. So their march was accomplished as a shuffle, each man holding onto the shoulder of the man in front as they walked in near blindness.

It took a couple of weeks, but in time their sight began to improve and recover its normal scope. Their eyes returned to their usual condition, the iris expanding back to normal size

Wyrdwood: The Story of Dusty Miller

and colour restored. But as a curious after-effect of this exposure to the nerve gas, an effect which persists to the present day, Dusty found that he could now see much better in the dark. This experiment and its initially distressing effects upon his eyes had somehow enhanced his night vision to a remarkable extent, also that of the other volunteers. This made them very useful as snipers, but has perhaps been even more useful to Dusty personally in civilian life. It assists him to see in the deep woods in low light conditions. Perhaps the Folks Upstairs prompted him to volunteer for this very reason.

Dusty stands amid immense Beech roots

Dusty's time in active service remained eventful as he was shot whilst in Cyprus. Fortunately, this 'bullet with his

Wyrdwood: The Story of Dusty Miller

name on it' missed his vitals and just grazed him. His father, Dusty Miller 12th, had prepared a runescript for him to keep him safe before he set off. At the moment the shot was fired, some intuition told Dusty that he had better move and as he turned, the bullet which would have killed him gave him a flesh wound instead. These intuitions and inner convictions are often the way in which magic works, when we suddenly know something and act upon it, without quite knowing how or why on a conscious level. In this instance, it saved Dusty's life, thanks to the influence of his father's runescript. We'll talk a lot more about runescripts later.

His period of service done, Dusty picked up his role and his family duties, carrying forward the work of the Dusty Millers, taking over from his father. He continued to work with LiveWood (see the next chapter) and to craft various magical items and runescripts which could be used to help people. Dusty has been known as a 'cudgel craftsman' and some of his larger sticks and staves certainly qualify as cudgels and the spells bound into them are usually defensive, the aim of such artefacts being to defend the home. It was in this capacity, as a maker of extraordinarily unique and evocative wands, cudgels and staves, that Dusty became increasingly well known.

Two or three decades ago, Dusty was a regular fixture at such English pagan events as the Prediction Festival, where he would meet people and talk with them about his work, offering his wares for sale to enhance the lives of those who passed by his stall, helping them to deal with any problems. It is significant that many of those people still recall their meetings with Dusty with fondness. Since I began writing this book and made my friends aware that I was doing it, several of them have made very positive comments to me: "He's a lovely guy and a real magician"; "He's a man of honour"; "I bought my first wand from Dusty some thirty years ago." It is very telling that there is such a large and warm feedback even from within my own small circle of friends (I had no idea prior to this that so many of them had crossed paths with Dusty in the past). So this should be some indicator of the impression he and his work have made on peoples' lives. As I mentioned earlier, he explained to me that the secret to being a witch is being in the right place to help people. Dusty has certainly achieved that.

Dusty Miller 13th

Wyrdwood: The Story of Dusty Miller

It is fascinating to trace the origins of Dusty's knowledge and to trace its development with the passing of generations to the present day. None of it is based upon book-learning. Until the time of his grandfather, Dusty Miller 11th, no one in his family was able to read. Although they have been able to consult books more recently and supplement their knowledge with information from other sources, the roots of the Old Religion and the ways of the Elf magic have been passed down by word of mouth. Dusty speaks of "the Folks Upstairs" rather than pinning those who listen to him speak down to any particular religious model. But within that broad category of "the Folks Upstairs", he and Dusty 14th identify four Gods and Goddesses of the Old Religion in particular who inform their work. These correspond to the Sun, the Moon, the Earth and the Sky; respectively Father, Mother, Grandmother and Grandfather. But we will look into this material more closely in a later chapter.

Dusty has been of assistance to a very large number of people in his long working life to date, some of whom are very well known. I am not going to betray any confidences or reveal any identities here, as Dusty is a man of great professional integrity. But a few of the tales deserve to be told nonetheless, to serve as illustrations of the ways in which he helps people.

We may consider the case of a man who was already very famous in his field, a regular face on our television screens. But he wanted to turn his hand to something new and become a novelist. Dusty provided him with the appropriate assistance to find his inspiration and bring his innermost skills to bear and the transition to author was a hugely successful one. It is important to note that Dusty doesn't work by giving you something for nothing. Instead, he enables you to realise and make the very best of the skills and abilities you already have, but may not yet have realised. This is a far more long-term benefit than any 'quick fix', and of far higher evolutionary and personal transformative value. We are all more than we seem and Dusty can draw our unseen potential out of us and display it for the world to see.

There was also the case of a famous radio and occasional television actor who approached Dusty and explained his problem to him. This gentleman was facing an audition before a film company, trying to sell them an idea for a character and situations which could lead to a series of movies. The problem was, so much was riding upon the success of this audition that he was really feeling the pressure. If he fouled it up, he would be jeopardising the livelihood of all the people – the crew, the assistants and the other actors – who were now committed to the project and dependent upon it going ahead and being a success. The responsibility was weighing him down because the decision which would affect so many people's futures revolved around his performance. He didn't need something to help him act well; he could already act well, he was at the top of his game. But he asked Dusty for something which would relieve him of the burden of pressure, so that he could simply walk into the audition without worrying and concentrate on acting to the best of his ability and giving a good pitch. The films he went on to make are listed among many people's favourites and were hugely successful. Sometimes it isn't so much that someone will need their abilities enhancing, but that they will need a worry or a blockage which is burdening them removed.

Another interesting and entertaining tale which Dusty tells and which illustrates the unique and sentient nature of the LiveWood items he creates, concerns a man who once bought a walking stick from him at a psychic fair. Some time later, shortly before the event finished, the man returned to Dusty's stall and said, "I seem to have lost my walking stick. I had it with me when I went to the toilet, but forgot to pick it up and take it with me when I left. I've just gone back in to look for it, but it isn't there."

Wyrdwood: The Story of Dusty Miller

"Well, nobody's handed it back in here," said Dusty. "Why don't you go back and check all of the cubicles this time?"

The man shortly arrived back and declared that the other cubicles were empty too.

"I see," said Dusty, "then you'd best check all of the other toilets on the premises. You'll find the walking stick again, I'm sure of it."

But the stick wasn't to be found in any of the toilets on the premises where the psychic fair was being held. "In that case," said Dusty, "I'm afraid a little work might be involved. You'll need to go around town tonight, checking in each public loo until you find it."

The customer was puzzled, but promised he'd do as Dusty said.

The following day, Dusty received a call from the man, who confirmed that he had spent the night checking around all the public lavatories in town and he had indeed discovered the misappropriated walking stick propped against the wall in one of them, where it had been abandoned by whoever had taken it.

"I knew that would happen," explained Dusty. "You see, the stick knew that you were its rightful owner and that the person who had taken it from the toilet had stolen it. Since he had stolen it in a toilet, the stick gave him the shits until he decided he'd had enough and left it in one himself."

The question of how the walking stick could possibly have known these things and acted upon them in this way will be answered in the next chapter.

One of the other interesting people Dusty has met through his work was Vicky Wall, who developed the range of Aura-Soma bottles. Able to see people's auras (the energy field that surrounds all living things) from an early age, Vicky Wall went blind mid-life, but found that although her eyes no longer saw the material world around her, she was still able to see and read auras. She went on to create a range of multi-layered

Wyrdwood: The Story of Dusty Miller

coloured waters, which she called Aura-Soma, designed to heal people's auric energies and restore them to balance and health. She met Dusty at a psychic fair when she approached his stall to see what she could read from the LiveWood auras. Dusty was overcome with emotion as he related how one piece in particular "reminded her of things she had forgotten". LiveWood chooses its owner, so naturally he gifted that piece to her.

Dusty Miller 13th in 1983

Wyrdwood: The Story of Dusty Miller

After many years living and working in Kent, Dusty moved to the Netherlands and spent several years living in Holland, where he was in great demand, giving talks on his work and making the LiveWood items available for people to examine and purchase. Whilst resident in Holland, a DVD was recorded, in which he explains his work in great detail. (A link to purchase this DVD will be provided in the 'Further Reading' at the close of the book.)

The house Dusty and his wife Jen inhabited in Holland was festooned with examples of LiveWood artefacts and was deliberately made to be an extension and an expression of Dusty's work.

Dusty remarks that there is a noticeable difference in the ways in which the Dutch and Germans approach the wands and other items he crafts, compared to the British and Americans and this was one of the reasons he moved to Holland, sensing the great enthusiasm and practical approach there. An American will tend to pick up one of the wands and examine it intently, saying, "Oh yes, this is very fascinating. I must take this home and put it on display. I think I'll hang it on my wall." An Englishman will tend to pick it up and then say, "What a wonderful thing. I shall have to go home and read a book about this to learn more about it. In fact, I may read two books." But a Dutchman will pick a wand up and then start gesturing with it and trying out different ways to hold and direct it, asking, "Can I do this with it? Can I use it in this way?" Dusty's response is always, "I don't know, you'll have to try it and see what happens for you as you bond with it." But this practical, dynamic interest was something he found very refreshing.

Dusty also had a feeling that Holland was centrally placed to be important in some of the changes he senses will be occurring in the world in the next two or three decades. He wanted to nurture a sense of readiness in these people who responded so enthusiastically to the information he had to share with them. These are matters we'll return to in the final chapter, where we will take a little time to look ahead.

In 2004, Dusty and his son Dusty 14th were acknowledged the last authentic native Shamen of Western Europe, when they were invited to take part in the 5th International Congress of Shamen and Healers, which was held at Mondsee in Austria. As the name suggests, this is a gathering of Shamen from around the world, from many different cultures which have individuals who exhibit a Shamanic sacred function.

Dusty 13th (seated 2nd from left) and Dusty 14th (seated far right) at the International Congress of Shamen and Healers

Dusty recalls that some of the fellow delegates took themselves very seriously indeed. So does he, of course, he believes totally in what he is doing and in the tremendous importance of his work. But he also intuitively understands that being po-faced is not the way to communicate the siginificance of that work to people.

The assembled Shamen were asked to speak a few words for a television programme which would feature the Congress. Some gave very fine speeches, presenting themselves as ambassadors for their culture and traditions. But when the two Dustys were asked to contribute, they linked arms and danced around, laughing. This delightful exhibition was broadcast on the television programme, lightening the tone considerably.

As Dusty explained to me, if people are seen to be having fun, it removes fear and tension. Shamen are strange and otherworldly characters and people in modern society are unsure about these seemingly odd people with odd beliefs and odd practices. But it is hard to feel fear or mistrust when people are seen to be making merry and having fun.

A couple of years ago, Dusty moved back to Kent, where he found the house where I met him, situated at the point where three Ley currents cross. He still goes out into the forest to gather the LiveWood when prompted by the Folks Upstairs and he still crafts wands and other items from it. He still gives talks on occasion. Now that he has returned here to England, it would be nice to think that there could be a rebirth of interest in all things Elfin in this country.

Dusty's 'eerie eyrie', at the top of his house, is the area where the Ley energy is most concentrated and where he carries out much of his work. This level of the house acts as a Faraday cage, gathering the energy for Dusty's use, but insulating it so that it doesn't inconvenience the neighbours. Only Dusty, his immediate family, and the Deities he refers to as the Folks Upstairs, have access to this level of the house. Dusty has his main computer up in this energised space and one curious effect of the Ley energy is that the wireless signal is totally lost here and he has to rely on a cable to connect it to his network. This absorption of electrical or wireless energy is a known side effect of high levels of psychic vibration.

Times are certainly changing, but this need not be to the detriment of folk like Dusty. Indeed, he has embraced the spirit of the times and used it to enhance the work he does and the way in which he reaches out to people, using modern communication systems to best possible advantage. He can also be much more open than his predecessors given the repeal of the anti-witchcraft laws in the middle of the last century. There is no longer the same need for discretion.

To put this in proper perspective, Dusty estimates that his father probably helped about thirty five people in his lifetime, but Dusty helps many more than that in a single month.

He is helped in this, of course, by his son Dusty 14th. Dusty 14th has inherited his grandfather's mechanical skills and is also a fully experienced Elfin craftsman in his own right. He tends to make the larger items now, such as staves and cudgels, since he has more space available than his father.

Many of the talks are now being given by Dusty Miller 14th, as he now takes his turn to explain Elfin philosophy to those who are eager to hear of it.

Dusty 14th is also very computer literate and is concerned with getting the message of the Elfin and the Dryads out to the world through the medium of the internet.

The opportunities for the expansion of consciousness, and a better understanding of humanity and the world in which we live, have never been greater. Similarly, however, the responsibility has never been greater. It is necessary to communicate these matters to people and it is necessary for people to listen and think in order to understand.

CHAPTER THREE

DRYADS: THE LIVING FOREST

One of the major things that distinguishes the Elfin philosophy and magick from that of others is the very special relationship they – as Tree Elves – have established with the trees of the forest. They not only live amongst the trees, but thanks to their great intuitive capacity and empathic awareness, they have always been very conscious of the trees as living beings.

Because, of course, trees **are** living beings. This is something which it is so easy for us to forget today, when trees seem no more than ornaments at the sides of roads, or embellishments to make the countryside look nice. Our modern preoccupation with manufactured things has tended to tragically lessen our consciousness of natural, living things.

But Dusty's family has never lost sight of the living forest, they are immersed in it. Moreover, they are aware that not only are trees alive, they are also sentient beings. Still further, they are sentient beings who can be communicated with. In fact, the Dusty Millers have been talking to the trees of their homeland for thousands of years, from time immemorial.

Trees have spirits just as humans do. As we possess an

invisible Higher Self, so do they. Although we have no common physical language or means of articulate communication, our Higher Selves are able to communicate with each other, if our minds are open enough to perceive and understand the exchange. You can try this by going and sitting down by a tree. You may choose to lean back against its trunk, you may like to press your hands or forehead against it, you may simply like to sit there and look at it. If it is a hollow tree, you might even venture inside it. But in whatever way feels right for you, settle down and focus your mind. Shut out all of the usual ceaseless rabbiting and internal chatter that passes through your brain and focus instead solely on the tree. Then, when your body and mind are still, you will be more alert to the promptings of your Higher Self. Reach out with your mind, thinking those thoughts you wish to communicate to the tree and be open to its response if there is one. There may not be a detailed response at first. You may not quite have attuned the 'knack' of listening, or the tree might be surprised and a little reticent that a human actually tries to speak with it. But if you persist with several trees, you will find that you begin to receive thoughts and impressions back in time, sometimes in pictures or feelings rather than in words. Most trees are quite interested in communicating and sharing with our species.

wyrdwood: The Story of Dusty Miller

Of course, since the Elfin folk lived among the trees and had naturally balanced and functional tricameral minds, we might expect them to have developed some fairly sophisticated and intricate communications over their long generations. This indeed proves to be the case, they have acquired a very detailed understanding of the life of trees and their spirits and a very close and unique relationship has grown up between Elfin Shamen and the trees they work with.

If you go around talking of trees and tree spirits, however, you will get only a nominal response. In time, they may come to know what you mean by such terms and respond to them, but it is an ancient magical principle that a thing will always respond best to its own name. This is only common sense really. You will respond much more readily and favourably if someone calls you by your proper name instead of just saying, "Hey, you over there in the dark coat." In the same way, tree spirits have a name which they collectively respond to, a term which best describes them. This name is a word from an Indo-European root which has variations in a few different languages, but which has come down to us as 'Dryad'. A tree spirit is properly termed a Dryad. This is the name they respond to and are alert to. In fact, Dusty would tell you that even as you read that last sentence and thought the word 'Dryad' in your mind, every tree in your locality will have become aware of you and will have taken an interest. This is because we communicate with them on a mental plane, where our Higher Selves may reach out and touch theirs. So you don't need to vocalise; just thinking the name 'Dryad' in your mind will immediately attract their attention.

But a Dryad is more than just a tree spirit. We humans are individuals and when we see a tree we tend to think of that as an individual too. We assume it is a thing in itself, separate from every other tree. But this is not actually the case. A single Dryad consciousness will be situated within a group of trees, not just in one tree. It will be able to perceive and communicate through each of the trees within its being. It would be possible to speak to a beech tree in one locality, then walk a hundred yards and find another beech tree and talk to that too, only to be speaking to the same Dryad. The Dryad itself possesses a consciousness in many ways similar to our own, but that consciousness is manifest throughout several 'bodies', not just the one. Of course, the trees which comprise a Dryad's 'body' or earthly anchor are not generally very mobile, they are rooted to the spot, and this may be a reason why their consciousness has developed in this particular way.

Tree Dryads

It is therefore often the case (though not invariably) that all of the trees of a certain type in a particular area will constitute a single Dryad. For example, all of the birch trees on one side of a river might be a single Dryad consciousness, whilst those on the other side will be another Dryad. It is equally possible that at some earlier time all of these birch trees might have formed one Dryad, but have since split into two. (We'll come back to Dryad methods of reproduction below, as these are very important when considering Dusty's work with them.)

Since a Dryad will never consist of multiple tree types, but is only one species of tree, and since the various kinds of trees are often mixed up and mingled with each other in a natural woodland, it will be apparent that there is a lot of overlapping between the Dryads, as Dryads of birch, oak, holly, hazel and so on will all inter-penetrate each others' energy fields. This close overlapping of trees' Higher Selves is quite natural and an important part of their communication and fellowship with each other.

Since the Dryads are manifest in several trees over an area, not just a single one, and since they all interpenetrate each other like overlapping fields of energy, how large are they? And what do they look like?

Wild Dryads

When asked this question, Dusty explains that he is 'aware' of the presence of Dryads, but they are not seen with the physical eyes, in the same way that our own inner thoughts and Higher Selves cannot be seen with the physical eyes. When we look at another human being, we only see their physical appearance with our eyes, and when we look at a Dryad, we only see the physical appearance of the group of trees that embodies them.

Since the consciousness of the Dryad is not a physical thing, it can vary greatly in perceived shape and size. When attuned to it, the mind perceives a Dryad as a field of thought energy, which extends across and around all of the trees which are connected to it. So it can appear to be a huge dome of energy which encircles and towers over these trees. They tend to seem very large indeed when in the wild, towering over the treetops, but their size is variable and they can also be tiny if they wish to be, shifting at will. Dusty speaks of how they have sometimes been envisioned as great, hooded gods of the forest, their heads and faces concealed by cowls, for they have no discernible features as we would understand them.

The Dustys with Dryad Friends

Dusty himself has drawn pictures of the Dryads, representing them as figures like gigantic, slightly formless ghosts of various hues towering over the forest below, all overlapping. He draws smiling, happy faces on his Dryads to show that they are beneficent and are happy to communicate with humans, but of course they don't actually have faces at all, nor do they look like this at all. His pictures are symbolic, intended to illustrate how the Dryads **feel** when he encounters them rather than how they look. He shows them in various diferent shades of colour, suggesting that the energy field of each Dryad may be tinted in certain ways to indicate its nature and its areas of expertise.

If the Dryads have no eyes, we need to ask how they can be aware of us? Are they able to see? They can see us after their fashion, but it might be more accurate to say that they can **sense** us. They possess senses other than sight. Their energy extends over the area surrounding their trees and is sensitive to vibrations within that area. Today we might liken it to a kind of radar, which detects all movement around a tree in a full 360° span. So it is impossible to sneak up on a tree, it will always sense you approaching long before you get there. In days gone by, this was presumed to be a result of having innumerable invisible eyes on all sides and gave birth to tales of the many-eyed gods who lived among the trees. But today we are better able to understand the existence of a field which picks up vibration and movement in a surrounding area.

Dryads are not sexually differentiated beings like humans and they reproduce by splitting, forming a clone copy of the original Dryad, complete with all of the same knowledge and memories. These two Dryads will then continue as separate entities, each leading their own life. This explains the comment I made earlier, where the groups of trees on either side of a river were each animated by a separate Dryad, but may at one time in the past have been a single Dryad. It will be seen that due to the great age of trees and their slow growth that Dryads will tend to clone themselves and reproduce only quite slowly under normal circumstances, as new trees appear and spread. There is one notable exception to this, however, when a clone will be deliberately formed for a specific purpose. But this is central to Dusty's work and will be addressed in the next chapter.

At some point, the question is bound to occur: why should we want to talk to trees? There are very good and rational reasons for doing so, but before I offer them, the most important reason is a deeper, more emotional one: it is good

Wyrdwood: The Story of Dusty Miller

and fulfilling to learn to communicate with other forms of life. The fact that something lives is in itself a good enough reason to wish to communicate and to learn from each other.

> This Sacred BEECH Tree (Beuk) is known as the 'Grandmother Tree' because of her lovely friendly vibrations. She is over 1,500 years old and was standing here in her Ley-Vortex when Charles the Great (Charlemagne) was busy founding the 'Holy Roman Empire'.
>
> My ancestors have been consulting her for many centuries now and we still do today. She supplies us with LiveWood for some of our Magical Tools.

Wyrdwood: The Story of Dusty Miller

Consider the great age of trees. Some of the Dryads that Dusty speaks with are thousands of years old. They have accumulated so much knowledge and wisdom over that time, observing the turning and transforming of the world, with all its patterns and cycles. They have had so much time to observe the processes of being and to meditate upon them. With our comparatively short lifespans and poor span of data, we are infants in comparison to them in these regards. Also, because of the nature of Dryads and the way in which a single consciousness is present within and around a group of trees, permeating the consciousness fields of other Dryads at the same time, they are more acclimatised to the spiritual dimensions than even the most intuitive of humans tend to be. So there is so much that we can learn from them.

Although Dryads have been around considerably longer than humans and often live for thousands of years, a curious phenomenon has taken place over the last century or two. Humans have suddenly started accelerating in their understanding of the world around them and their practical application of its laws. Human progress and technology is advancing at an incredible rate and overtaking the Dryads in some areas, despite our comparative youth as a species and comparatively short lives. So we have knowledge to share with the Dryads too.

There is also the fact that humans are individual, independent organisms, whereas a Dryad has its physical being spread across a number of trees. It may be that they are wishing to progress towards an evolution promoting greater individualism and can gain the impetus for this from we humans.

So Dryads and humans can be of mutual help to each other. This is accomplished not only by direct communication, but also by assistance in magick and spiritual works. But this will be explained in the next chapter.

Dusty's family have discovered that although many

trees can be talked with, those which tend to be most communicative and most willing to offer tangible assistance to mankind are those which grow in areas with a strong concentration of Leylines. The area of Kent in which Dusty lives has a large number of Leylines (witness the three that pass through his own house), so it is a place well suited to his work.

There are no fewer than sixty groups of trees in the region surrounding Dusty's home who are willing to speak with him and to assist him (and through him, humanity as a whole). That's sixty Dryads, each of which is resident in a particular group of trees. These are the Dryads who offer practical help to humanity in the form of LiveWood, and who see and experience more of the world through their association with humans in return.

Dusty's people soon realised that all trees have a certain energy associated with them and that many of them are willing to share this energy with humans they trust. There are two main types of energy emanating from trees. Some of them extend a warm, revitalising energy that recharges the batteries and gives a good energy boost when you need it. Since this type of energy reminded the Elf-folk of the Sun, it is termed **Sola** energy. The other type of energy is cooler and more reflective and introspective and is good for relieving stress and reaching a state of calm. Because this is reminiscent of the Moon, it is called **Luna** energy.

Dusty has also taken on board the research of famed British dowser, the late Tom Lethbridge, whose quiet and open-minded studies made many startling discoveries in the field of dowsing, not least the fact that different materials and properties responded to different pendulum rates, measured by the length of the string to which the weight was attached. Dusty has thus been able to go on to determine the pendulum rates not only for different types of tree, but also for different tribes within the same species. (We'll return to Tom

Lethbridge and his fascinating research in a later chapter.)

Wyrdwood: The Story of Dusty Miller

If you know the type of energy a given kind of tree expresses, you will be able to go into the woods and locate a tree which can help you when you need it. You can get a little pick me up by sitting leaning against a Sola tree, allowing its warmth and vibrancy to suffuse your being. Or you can spend some time with a Luna tree if you need to soothe your frustrations and clear your head. The following tables (overleaf) list many different kinds of tree, divided into the Sola and Luna categories, so you can find out which grow in your own neighbourhood and seek them out. Their Lethbridge pendulum rates are also given, as some may find it a fascinating exercise to investigate these further.

Wyrdwood: The Story of Dusty Miller

Sola Trees

English Name:	Latin Name:	Rate:
Almond	Prunus dulcis	5"
Ash	Fraxinus excelsior	6"
Quaking Aspen	Populus tremula	8"
Silver Birch	Betula pendula	38"
Horse Chestnut	Aesculus hippocastanum	16"
Lawson Cypress	Chamaecyparis lawsoniana	34"
Dogwood	Thelycrania sanguinea	6"
Elder	Sambucus nigra	9"
English Elm	Ulmus procera	23"
Silver Fir	Abies alba	8"
Holly	Ilex aquifolium	38"
Laburnham	Laburnum anagyroides	22"
Locust Tree	Robinia pseudacacia	39"
Field Maple	Acer campestre	11½"
Mulberry	Morus nigra	7"
Common Oak	Quercus robur	11"
Pine	Pinus sylvestris	31"
Lombardy Poplar	Populus nigra italica	16"
Black Poplar	Populus nigra	8"
Giant Redwood	Sequoiadendron giganteum	6"
Sycamore	Acer pseudoplatanus	9"
White Willow	Salix alba	9"
Walnut	Juglans regia	11"
Irish Yew	Taxus fastigiata	28"

Wyrdwood: The Story of Dusty Miller

Luna Trees

English Name:	Latin Name:	Rate:
Alder	Alnus glutinosa	12"
Snakeskin Ash	Fraxinus angustifolia	6"
Beech	Fagus sylvatica	17"
Blackthorn	Prunus spinosa	11½"
Box	Boxus sempervirens	32"
Cherry	Prunus avium	12"
Sweet Chestnut	Castanea sativa	39"
Crab Apple	Malus sylvestris	18"
Damson	Prunus domestica	12½"
Douglas Fir	Pseudotsuga menziesii	37"
Downy Birch	Betula pubescens	38"
Forsythia	Forsythia suspensa	12"
Hazel	Corylus avellana	20½"
Hornbeam	Carpinus betulus	24"
Larch	Larix decidua	38"
Linden/Lime	Tilia vulgaris	31"
Norway Maple	Acer platanuides	12"
May/Whitethorn	Crataegus monogyna	5½"
Sessile Oak	Quercus petraea	33"
Turkey Oak	Quercus cerris	24"
Pin Oak	Quercus palustris	11"
Red Oak	Quercus rubra	22"
Pear	Pyrus communis	32"
Plane	Platanus hispanica	23"
Plum	Prunus domestica	12½"
Rowen	Sorbus aucuparia	13"
Wild Service	Sorbus torminalis	6"
Snowy Mespil	Amelanchier ovalis	34½"
Spindle	Euonymus europaeus	21"
Spruce	Picea abies	32"
Water Elder	Viburnum opulus	13"
Whitebeam	Sorbus aria	7"
Goat Willow	Salix caprea	7"
English Yew	Taxus Baccata	28"

Having established which trees belong in which category, Dusty has begun cataloguing the general characteristics of each kind of tree and the Dryad consciousness that manifests through them. He has found it useful to picture each species of Dryad in terms of some human archetype, as this makes it easier for people to understand them.

This task of classification and description is still very much a work in progress, but the common tree-tribe types and their personality characteristics which have been discovered and described so far are detailed below. As Dusty 14th pointed out to me, this list is a guideline only, as the Dryads of different kinds are observing the work done through the LiveWood tools crafted from other varieties, and they are evidently starting to learn from each other, becoming more multi-talented!

YEW

"The Wise Old Man of the Woods" or "The Grandfather"
Luna, 28"

Yew Dryads tend to exhibit a character similar to Merlin, the kingmaker and wizard of the Arthurian tales, the real power behind the throne.

In many ways, yew is like a teacher, whose speciality is teaching right-brain concepts in left-brain terms, allowing creativity and intuition to be grasped by the intellect and thus channeled into a positive plan of action.

This tree-tribe specialises in healing, magick and philosophy and teaches these things to those humans who will listen and converse with it.

Wyrdwood: The Story of Dusty Miller

BEECH

"The Wise Old Lady of the Woods" or "The Grandmother"
Luna, 17"

Do you remember when you were young and you used to run to your Granny for comfort whenever something troubled you? (For grandmothers are much more indulgent than parents.) Beech is like that Granny, relaxing and soothing you and allowing you a space in which you can calm down and regain your emotional bearings.

A wise and calm advisor and friend.

Dusty explained how he has seen many trees of the Grandfather and Grandmother type who have grown roots or branches almost like laps or knees to sit upon.

OLIVE

Another "Grandmother"
Luna, 17"

Very similar characteristics to beech.

LINDEN

Another "Grandmother"
Luna, 31"

Very similar characteristics to beech and olive.

Wyrdwood: The Story of Dusty Miller

HAZEL

"The Magician" or "The Whizz-Kid"
Luna, 20$^1/_2$"

Hazel Dryads are natural Shamen, adept at magick, healing and the development of mental abilities. Hazel has long been considered the choice par excellence for dowsing rods and is featured as a wood for magical wands and other items in many legends and folk-tales.

Hazel is a very good teacher, who makes things happen and gets things done.

ROWAN

"The Quicken" or "The Yuppie"
Luna, 13"

As the name would suggest, the rowan is a very lively and vigorous tree, a bit of a magical whizz-kid, just like hazel. A tree which encourages rapid, decisive action and quick-thinking.

Rowan is also concerned with teaching the meaning of the difficult and sometimes painful lessons we all have to learn in life and specialises in bringing out the best in people.

HOLLY

"The Priest" or "Spiritual Leader"
Sola, 38"

The 'Winter Lord' of the Celts, holly is an enthusiastic spiritual leader and will assist greatly in your spiritual development.

Holly possesses a strong positive vibe and is very energetic, boosting and improving the mental attitude of everyone it interacts with.

HORNBEAM

"The Strong Right Arm" or "The Henchman"
Luna, 24"

Hornbeam is a very faithful and trustworthy tree, who will stick by you and assist you. It understands what it is that you are trying to do and will do its best to make it happen for you.

The tree extends loyalty and protection and offers its assistance in all your endeavours.

COMMON OAK

"The Goodman" or "Salt of the Earth"
Sola, 11"

The oak is strong, reliable and trustworthy. The names given to this tree in Indo-European languages tend to echo these characteristics, deriving from a root meaning 'steadfastness', 'truth' and 'troth'.

The oak doesn't display a lot of initiative or think for itself, but will diligently do as it is told, working solidly and consistently without supervision. It is a tree with great stamina and paces itself well, continuing steadily for long periods.

All the Sola oaks, i.e. English (11"), Cork (11"), and

Holm (33") have these 'Goodman' characteristics.

DURMAST OAK

"The Goodwife" or "Village Wise Woman"
Luna, 33"

A very capable and mature tree, sharing the steadfast and enduring qualities of the Sola oaks given above.

She acts as the village wise woman or midwife, bringing the children of her community into the world and working hard to keep them healthy throughout their life. When they die, it is she who prepares them for burial.

All of the Luna oaks, i.e. Sessile (33"), Red (22"), Pin (11"), Moss (11"), Turkey (24"), American (22"), and Evergreen (33") have these 'Wise Woman' characteristics.

ASH

"The Good Servant"
Sola, 6"

Ash is a very flexible and adaptable tree, but also capable of great precision. But it also needs to be told exactly what to do, as ash doesn't like to think for itself or to improvise, it requires clear, unambiguous instructions.

ELM

"The Supporter" or "Crutch"

Sola, 23"

The elm provides a tremendous level of supportive energy. It is strong to lend its assistance to your work when you are beginning to flag, adding its own strength to yours. It provides a solid foundation when all around seems unstable and fragile. Something to lean on.

ASPEN

"The Trembler"
Sola, 8"

Aspen is a natural pacifist, one who provides defence by appearing to be non-threatening, thus a passive form of defence (hence the 'trembling' of its boughs and leaves).

Its pacifism and desire to avoid or circumvent trouble or confrontation wherever possible should not be taken to imply it is weak. It is actually possessed of great strength when the need arises.

WILLOW

"Sympathetic Sally"
Luna, 7" & 9"

Willow is a very empathic tree. These Dryads feel your pain and share the experience of your troubles, so are well placed to steer you through them, comforting and guiding you. Sympathy and support from one who truly knows how you feel and what you are going through, and who has the insight to put matters back on a good footing. All willows seem to share these characteristics.

PINE

"The Macho Show-Off" or "Poser"
Sola, 31"

Pine is strong, boisterous and unapologetic, leading from the front. This tree will charge headlong into any situation and carry out orders to the letter, every inch the macho action hero. But as is often the case with such personality types, pine feels no responsibility for the consequences of its actions as long as it has accomplished what it was asked to do. This leaves the balance factor and considerations of possible collateral damage in your own hands and judgement.

So a very effective and dynamic soldier, but needs to be handled with care and precision.

BLACKTHORN

"The Constable" or "Law-Enforcer"
Luna, 11$^1/_2$"

Blackthorn is an absolute moralist, who sticks to the rules rigidly, refusing to bend them in any way, shape or form. It expects you to behave in the same manner and will refuse to co-operate if you do not. It acknowledges no viewpoint but its own and what it deems to be 'right' according to the laws of nature.

As such, it is a valuable and determined ally and

prosecutor when you have been wronged, but you need to be sure of the justice of your own case.

WHITETHORN

"The Nun" or "The Vestal Virgin"
Luna, 5½"

As the above titles suggest, whitethorn's character suggests a woman devoted to religious service, in this case to the Goddess. (We'll take a look at the Old Religion in a little more detail later in the book.)

Whitethorn's duties are in the fields of teaching and self-development and she is a very skilled and accomplished healer.

ELDER

"The Look-Out" or "Officer of the Watch"
Sola / Luna 9"

Elder is possessed of a Sola mind in a Luna body and appears as a lookout or a baby-sitter, a strong protective influence who keeps a very close eye over its wards.

Elder is very vigilant and ever alert for approaching danger. It will not allow any harm to befall those who are under its watch.

Wyrdwood: The Story of Dusty Miller

WILD APPLE

"The Round Lover"
Luna, 18"

WILD PEAR

"The Long Lover"
Luna, 32"

Both of these popular fruit trees are very loving and forgiving personalities. They will do everything in their power to nurture you, soothe away your doubts and insecurities, and make you feel good.

SILVER BIRCH

"The Carer"
Sola, 38"

DOWNEY BIRCH

"The Nurse"
Luna, 38"

These two trees are at the midpoint between Sola and Luna and their speciality is day to day nursing and care. They are very dedicated when it comes to nursing people with long term illnesses or who are terminally ill.

SNOWY MESPIL

"The Hard Worker"
Luna, 34$^{1}/_{2}$"

As the title suggests, you can call upon this tree with confidence to put in a great deal of effort. It will apply itself wholeheartedly toward doing a good job, putting in the maximum of effort with the minimum of supervision.

LARCH

"The Sports Coach"
Luna, 38"

This tree excels at helping and training you to make the most of your own abilities. It will work gently but persistently to teach you to rely upon and develop your skills, leading you to one small victory after another until you attain full confidence in yourself.

It encourages self-esteem, self-confidence and self-reliance, but backs it up by actively developing the abilities to support these feelings.

OLIVE

"The Home-Maker"
Luna, 39"

The atmosphere and 'homeliness' of where you live can have a profound effect upon your mood, your comfort, your energy levels and your general well-being. Olive understands this and concentrates and focuses upon making the home into a happy and supportive environment, with all of the benefits that this brings.

WALNUT

"The Leader of the Pack"
Sola, 11"

Walnut is possessed of a competitive, energetic nature that always goes full on for gold and will not accept second best. It will not allow anyone or anything to get in its way and must always be first in everything. So if you want to have something done first and done best, walnut is a good choice. Bear in mind that it does the tree good to be beaten just occasionally, to maintain its edge.

QUINCE

"The Tutor"
Luna, 31"

This tree is a great aid in studying and passing examinations. It is like a university professor, explaining things carefully and ensuring that its students gain a proper comprehension of the subject on a deep level. Patient, precise and persistent, it knows how best to arrange and order information in the mind.

Wyrdwood: The Story of Dusty Miller

FORSYTHIA

"The Good Companion"
Luna, 12"

This tree is very friendly and fun to have around. It can be of assistance in breaking the ice at social events, encouraging good company and building friendships. A boon for the shy.

This list is not exhaustive, of course, covering only a selection of trees. This is because the characteristics recorded here have been discovered by experience, through the process of actually working with the Dryads. They have not simply been assumed or copied from other sources. As such, there remain many trees to be added to this list, and probably qualities still to be discovered relating to the tree-types already on it.

It should also be noted that Dryads within a particular species may well exhibit personal traits which modify the general characteristics which are recorded here. We are dealing with sentient, living beings, after all, not with spreadsheets. It is essential to get to know any Dryad you work with personally in order to learn each other's talents and limits and establish a good working relationship.

How exactly does Dusty work with the Dryads, though? What is this LiveWood that has been referenced here and there in this chapter? What can the Dryads do for us, and why, and what can we do for them in return? These are all questions which need to be answered in the next chapter.

Wyrdwood: The Story of Dusty Miller

CHAPTER FOUR

CRAFTING THE LIVING WOOD

In previous chapters, I have made several references to 'LiveWood' and have mentioned that Dusty makes various pendants and wands from the wood of the trees that he works with. These items are of a most remarkable efficacy, each one possessing a spirit of its own, quite unlike any mass-produced tools you may have seen for sale in an occult mail order catalogue. Every item is unique and every item is sentient in its own right.

I can testify personally to the powerful nature of Dusty's craftsmanship. As I sit here typing this now, I am wearing a disc of elder around my neck which functions as an impenetrable psychic shield. It has also dipped into my thoughts and calmed me down on more than one occasion when I have been in danger of losing my temper over trivial matters. And I mean, quite literally, it communicated with me and restored my sense of perspective. Close to hand is my wand, a length of oak which is rounded at one end and hooked at the other. This wand has healing qualities all of its own and also amplifies and focuses my thoughts in ways that I have never been able to manage on my own. This is the wand I spoke of in the introduction which gave me a real physical jolt

Wyrdwood: The Story of Dusty Miller

when I first handled it. It is a huge support in my work. I also have a rune-inscribed disc of elder that is intended to provide safety and ease whilst travelling. Not only does it guarantee my safety and well-being when flying, it also seems to have the uncanny knack of making travel connections happen at exactly the right times and shortening my journey times in practice!

The thing that makes Dusty's items so different from others is that they are living and sentient; they are made from LiveWood. And as far as Dusty is aware, he and his family are the last people of the the aboriginal Elfin tribes still working with the Dryads and producing LiveWood artifacts. I guess it's therefore time for us to define exactly what LiveWood is and why it is so different from other kinds of wood.

We can define four different types of wood for the purposes of this discussion. All wood can be placed in one of these categories, regardless of the type of tree it comes from:

Living Wood: This is wood which is part of a living tree, growing in the ground. Whether root, branch or trunk, it is part of the tree's functioning organism and is enlivened by the Dryad who is manifest in the group of trees of which this one is part.

Dead Wood: This is wood which has been 'rejected' by a tree and which has withered and ultimately fallen to the ground. Trees will often reject a branch for whatever reason and withdraw the life force from it, whereupon it will die and drop off, it's a perfectly natural process. This kind of wood is good only for rotting down and feeding the other plants on the forest floor, or perhaps for gathering for fuel by humans, as was more frequently the case when most people had real fires in their hearths.

Greenwood: This is wood that has been cut from trees and prepared and preserved so that it can be shaped and used by carpenters and other artisans, who craft it into tables, chairs and so forth. This wood no longer carries any life force, there is no spirit in it, but because of the way it has been treated and prepared, it does not immediately rot and is a usable resource. All wooden items made by humans are of this type, including wooden artifacts sold by most occult suppliers.

LiveWood: LiveWood is the type of wood used exclusively by Dusty. This is wood which has been cut from the tree, but which still contains a living spirit and is sentient. All of Dusty's wands, pendants, cudgels and other items are made from LiveWood.

To understand how LiveWood retains the spirit of the wood within it, think back to the previous chapter, where it was explained how Dryads reproduce. They do this by splitting, by cloning themselves. When Dusty collects LiveWood by cutting it from a tree, the Dryad of the tree donates a clone of itself, which abides within the piece of wood which has been taken. The clone is an exact replica of the original Dryad, with the same memories and abilities, but from this point on it will live a separate life, housed within the piece of LiveWood which has been taken from the tree.

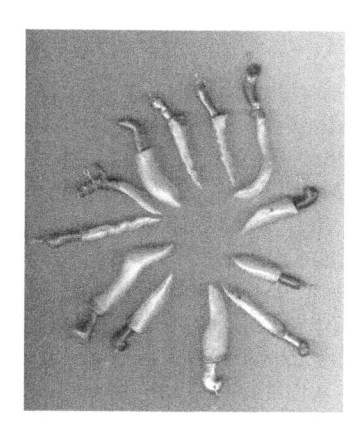

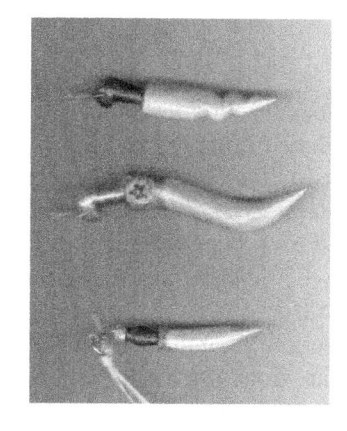

wyrdwood: The Story of Dusty Miller

It's not as simple as that, though. Dusty can't simply take himself out into the forest and start lopping off likely looking bits of wood that happen to take his fancy. These LiveWood limbs are purpose grown and when the tree has created an appropriate piece of wood, the Dryad needs to create the clone of itself and centre it in that particular part of the tree. The Dryads work with the Folks Upstairs just as much as the Elf-folk do, and they create these specially grown roots and branches as the Folks Upstairs instruct them to do so. Naturally, this is a process that often begins many years before Dusty comes to collect the wood when it is fully grown and suitable for its purpose.

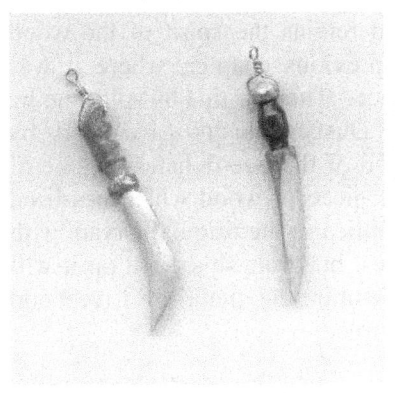

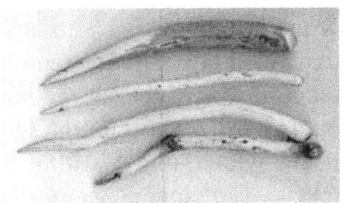

But even then, Dusty does not simply set out into the woods with an eye open for interesting pieces to collect. The whole process is directed by the Folks Upstairs, from instructing the Dryad to grow a suitable branch to furnish a healing wand, to instructing Dusty to go and collect the grown LiveWood and shape it into its ultimate form.

What happens from Dusty's point of view is that he will be quietly getting on with his own business when he will feel the prompting of his Higher Self that there is a message for him from the Folks Upstairs. He will then settle down and

Wyrdwood: The Story of Dusty Miller

focus his mind to receive that message, which will tell him that there is some LiveWood ready to be collected. Dusty will ask where the wood is to be found (he works with some sixty groups of active trees and their Dryads, covering quite a large area of ground). He will then be shown a vision of the area he is to go to (this will be a view of the area from high above it, looking down upon it at an angle). This will enable him to see roughly where he needs to go. He will then ask when the LiveWood is to be gathered and he will be shown a vision of the correct phase of the Moon, which will generally be three or four days from the time that he receives the summons.

When the appointed day arrives, Dusty rises very early in the morning and sets out to the forest at about 6:00 am. He drives to the area he was shown in the vision. (Recognising this can sometimes be a bit of a trial in itself, since the viewpoint of the vision is looking down from above, but the forest looks very different when you're actually down among the trees.) Once he is certain he is in the right place, Dusty says to the Folks Upstairs, "Right, I'm here. Now where do you want me to go?"

He will then receive an impression from them in reply, generally something along the lines of, "Look for a tree that is this shape", accompanied by a visual impression. He then looks around until he spots the tree of that particular shape, then says "Right, I can see that," and makes his way over to it. He then continues following directions of this type until he reaches the first tree which has LiveWood ready to collect.

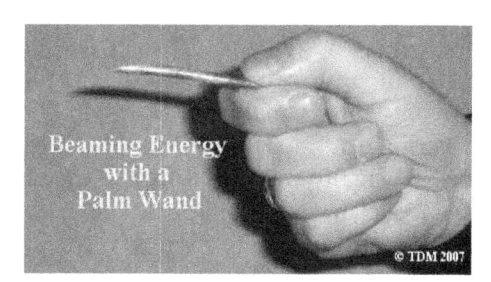

Beaming Energy with a Palm Wand

© TDM 2007

Wyrdwood: The Story of Dusty Miller

When Dusty examines this tree, he will notice that the branches, roots or other parts which are to be collected are clearly marked for him. Although there are no physical markings visible, his inner eye can discern a psychic marker. A kind of sparkling, silvery line seems to show the exact point at which he is to cut. This is at a precise point which will not hurt the tree. The parent Dryad is concentrated in the tree itself and does not extend beyond that mark into the piece of wood which is to be removed, so it will not be harmed. Similarly, the cloned Dryad is concentrated in the piece which will be removed and does not extend past the mark from that direction. So the point actually identified by the 'ghost light' is effectively numb and can be cut without paining the Dryads, like an umbilical cord joining parent and child.

Dusty uses incredibly sharp saws for the purpose of cutting. These tools are manufactured in Japan and the saw teeth are sharpened on both sides. He estimates that although they might snag a little on the bone, they would probably remove a limb in a single swift swoop. So he is very careful to ensure that accidents don't happen.

There have been occasions when Dusty has slipped and cut a tree in the wrong place, though, and he rolled up his trouser leg to show me some of the scars he bears. If he makes a mistake and hurts the tree, then he can be assured that the saw will slip and hurt him in his turn, to teach him his lesson. Collecting LiveWood, it can be seen, is a skilled and very delicate process.

He doesn't just gather a single piece of wood at a time, however. The Folks Upstairs plan ahead and ensure that a number of different pieces of LiveWood will all be coming ready for gathering at the same time. So when Dusty goes out on his early morning mission, he ensures he has a sack with him. This sack is usually pretty full by the time he gets back home, after being led from landmark to landmark, visiting in turn each tree that has wood ready for use.

Wyrdwood: The Story of Dusty Miller

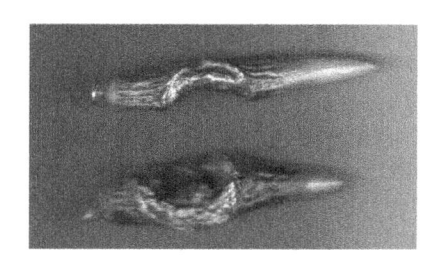

    The gathered LiveWood isn't ready to use immediately, of course. There are two distinct processes of preparation that it has to go through first, and these can take some considerable time.

    The wood itself must be dried out, as when freshly cut it is still full of sap. To this end, it is stored in Dusty's basement, standing upright in suitable containers (larger pieces are stored at Dusty 14th's home). Once a month or so, Dusty will go down into the basement to turn the wood over, from top to bottom, ensuring the process is a uniform one.

    While this is going on with the physical piece of wood, the Dryad inhabiting it is in a state of slumber, a kind of suspended animation. Although it possesses all of the memories of the Dryad it was cloned from, it has not yet learned all that it needs to for the task that now lies ahead of it. So while the wood is going through its period of drying and preparation, the Dryad's Higher Self is projected into the spiritual realms. Here it receives its training in the use of the powers it will exercise and harness when the LiveWood is finally activated. It meditates and gains in strength while it

Wyrdwood: The Story of Dusty Miller

sleeps, accumulating magical knowledge and ability, as well as a sense of purpose. The Dryad must learn what it is being sent into the world to achieve.

Dusty has developed a good sense for these things over the many years he has been working with LiveWood, and he is skilled at communicating with Dryads. So when he goes down into the basement to carry out his monthly turning of the wood, he can tell by touch when one of the pieces of LiveWood is beginning to stir from its slumber. That piece will then be set aside and he will keep coming back to it until he senses that it is fully awake and that the Dryad is now resident and alert within the wood, ready to begin its task.

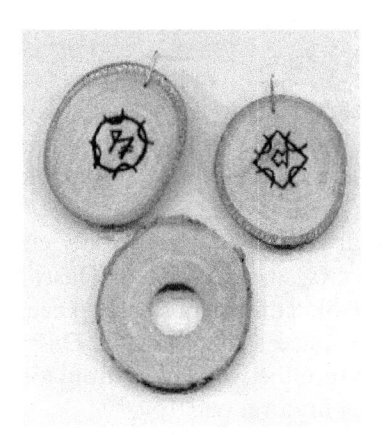

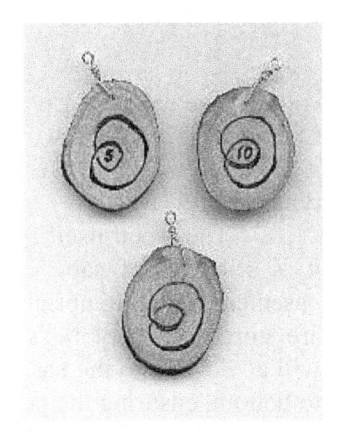

Before the LiveWood is ready to begin its work, however, it must be fashioned into an appropriate tool. The Dryad now knows what its function and purpose is and the wood is now dried and usable, but it must first be shaped into a suitable abode for the Dryad to carry out its task and interface with its ultimate human companion.

So Dusty takes up his tools and prepares to shape the wood into its ultimate form. At this stage he does not personally have any idea how the finished item will appear,

Wyrdwood: The Story of Dusty Miller

because he is adamant that it is not him that decides. He simply provides the hands through which the Folks Upstairs can work, directing him how to cut and mark and tint and polish until they are satisfied with what has been created.

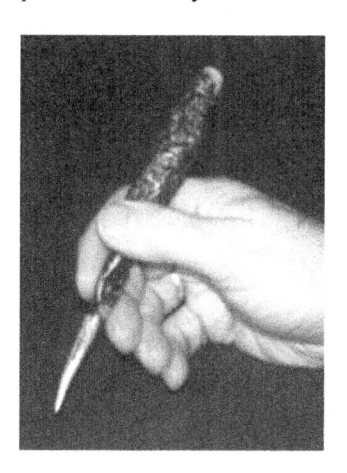

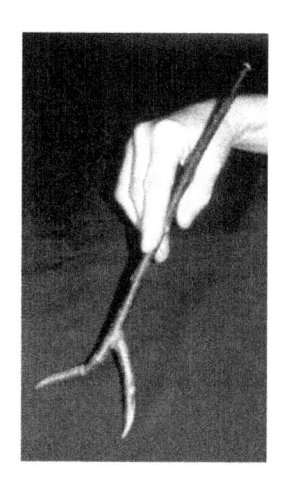

The Dryad is not present in the wood when Dusty shapes it. Instead, it projects itself out, putting itself in a kind of sleep, similar to a human being put under anaesthetic for an operation. Its Higher Self attaches itself to Dusty's, piggybacking his own Higher Self, and then both are moved and guided by the Folks Upstairs in the process of shaping the LiveWood. Wands, pendants, cudgels: all must be carved and smoothed and polished until they are fit for their purpose, until finally Dusty is told that the task is done. The Dryad re-enters the LiveWood artifact and Dusty is left holding the finished tool in his hands.

Even when it is complete, however, Dusty can really only guess what its purpose is, or how it is intended to be used. He is not at all put out by this, as he explains that since the item is not intended for him, there is no need for him to know. Nevertheless, he can make a fairly good assumption about the

Wyrdwood: The Story of Dusty Miller

general type of object it is. As we saw in the previous chapter, Dusty has succeeded in identifying the main characteristics of many trees and this will assist him in understanding what a tool made from that wood will be for. Similarly, its size and shape will be suggestive to him and over the years he has developed a fine intuition, so that he can readily tell when a tool is intended for healing, for example. But the finer details of its precise application are not his to know. These are secrets to be learned by the ultimate owner, or perhaps companion would be a better word, of the Dryad.

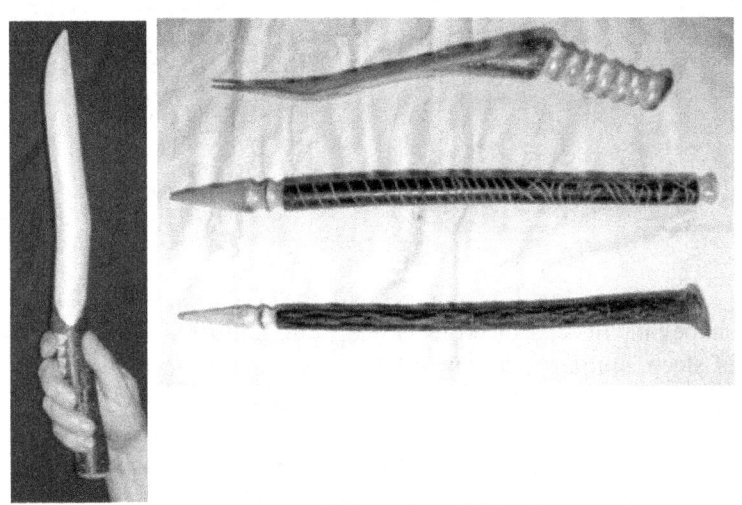

A LiveWood Sword and Wands

Who is the ultimate owner of a LiveWood tool? It's not just some random passer-by who happens to take a fancy to a wand at one of Dusty's talks. Dusty firmly believes that every piece of LiveWood he crafts is destined for a particular person, to meet a particular need. This should not be too surprising when we consider that the whole process is governed by the Folks Upstairs, who exist outside of our

Wyrdwood: The Story of Dusty Miller

bounded realm of time and space. Their foreknowledge and influence is perfectly capable of arranging things in this manner.

This raises fascinating questions about time as well. Since trees grow relatively slowly, they may start growing a special branch especially for the purpose of providing a piece of LiveWood many years before it will actually be needed. Indeed, in many cases, they begin growing a particular branch for a particular purpose before its recipient is even born.

Dusty has often known a piece of finished LiveWood to lie idle for quite a long time until the right person comes along, someone who has been earnestly looking for that precise thing. They will go directly to that particular Dryad, expressing how they just 'knew' that it was for them. Dusty suggests that this affinity between a human and a Dryad is similar to what happens when someone visits a litter of puppies with a view to buying one. They may pretend to look over all the pups, but there is always one who directly approaches them when they first arrive, bonding with them immediately, and this is the pup who has an affinity with them and is invariably the one they end up leaving with. It is the same with humans and Dryads; an affinity is there, a relationship already exists on an innermost level between the LiveWood and its intended owner. I have already explained in the introduction my own reaction when I picked up the wand that was meant for me.

Wyrdwood: The Story of Dusty Miller

This special relationship also determines the way in which a LiveWood tool is to be used. This is something that will be developed and fine-tuned by the human and Dryad as they work together and get to know each other. Dusty cannot tell you how to hold your wand or what precisely it can do. This is something you will learn by interacting with the Dryad, responding intuitively to its prompting. It is a particular delight to Dusty when people come back to him, letting him know what they have done with the assistance of their Dryad companion, how they have used it.

Dusty gives a talk, assisted by a LiveWood Staff

Wyrdwood: The Story of Dusty Miller

   Although a given wand may have a certain general label, such as 'healing', the way in which a particular Dryad will function is utterly unique to that Dryad and the human with whom it works. It may prompt its user to move it in certain ways, tracing certain symbols or making gestures. It may be pointed or held aloft. It may heal gently or by provoking crisis moments. It may heal from within or deal with the rapid treatment of symptoms. It may heal the mind or the body. Some Dryads are calming, others are invigorating (respectively Luna and Sola in nature, as discussed in the previous chapter). My own wand has a hooked point for tracing symbols and directing precise currents of energy, but at its other end it has a curved bulb which beams out a cone of stabilising, healing energy in a much more gentle fashion. Every piece of LiveWood is unique in its precise purpose and application. Some do not even have to be held. Dusty's range of 'Witch's Pocket Wands' are designed to be small enough to sit in the pocket, channeling their power through their user's hands and body, where it can be discreetly directed where required.

   The usefulness of these magical LiveWood tools to us humans is thus undoubted. But at some point the more discerning of Dusty's clients will always begin to wonder just what exactly the Dryad gets out of the deal? The provision of a living wood artifact with a spirit resident within it is a huge gift to humanity, but what do we have to do to fulfill our side of the bargain? What does humanity gift to the Dryads?

   The answer is quite simply that we provide our mobility. As we carry the LiveWood around, using it to work wonders, the Dryad is learning more about us and the world than it ever could when bound to a group of trees in a single location, no matter how expansive and communicative that group may be. The Dryad in the LiveWood travels around, learns about the wide world, and reports back to the Dryad from which it was cloned, and to which it remains intimately psychically linked. That Dryad then shares this information and insight with the other trees of the forest, catalysing and accelerating the development of Dryad consciousness.

One of the small LiveWood cudgels that Dusty wears on a cord around his neck is in permanent communication with its parent tree, which is one of the oldest trees which Dusty speaks with. So that very ancient and wise tree is privy to everything that Dusty says and does. It knows how the Shaman of the Elves is carrying out his work and how he is representing the Dryads in the world of humans. This realisation should go some way to explaining the great responsibility that Dusty bears.

A Display of Dusty's LiveWood Wares

This whole question is actually a profound one which makes us aware of the stakes. The exchange between human and Dryad which is embodied in the provision of LiveWood and the mediation of the Dusty Miller line of Shamen is not a simple curiosity. It is actually something of great importance to the spiritual evolution of two sentient species. That surely gives us something to think upon.

It is interesting to think about the similarities and differences between LiveWood tools and the tools created by other magical means by magicians and witches down through the ages. Because there are some obvious similarities, but the difference is a crucial one.

I have worked with the runes for a long time and if I want to make a runic tool – whether a talisman for a specific purpose, or a long term tool such as a wand – I will begin by selecting the correct material for the purpose. This will almost inevitably be wood (though I may select stone or metal for very long-term items). Wood is a perfect receptacle, since it is an organic substance which is capable of holding a living charge. But the wood that I – and other such runeworkers and magicians – use is not LiveWood. It is wood that was once alive, but is now simply a preserved shell, separated from the life force that once inhabited it.

So I prepare my runes and cut them into the wood, but they are not active and they are not alive. In order to activate the runes, I then have to colour them with red ink, whilst singing the runesongs into the carved shapes in the wood. In order to bring the tool to life, giving it the intelligence to carry out its purpose, I add some of my blood to the red ink. In other words, I have to put some of my own life force – both physical and psychic – into the tool I am making in order to activate it.

This stands in stark contrast to Dusty's LiveWood items, which are already alive and sentient, each one containing a Dryad. Certainly, if we look back through the annals of occultism it is possible to find reference to magicians who have bound Elemental spirits into material objects and so forth, but this too is a wholly different kettle of fish to the covenant we see between Elf and Dryad, made manifest in Dusty's work. For this represents a benevolent and mutually rewarding agreement between two species, designed to complement the spiritual development of each. It is absolutely unique in that respect.

My own runic carvings are perfectly effective within their limits, but they can never be as flexible and adaptable as LiveWood tools. The presence of a living, thinking Dryad within each wand, cudgel or pendant, means that it is capable of assessing and adapting to a situation on the fly; it is not dependent upon a human operator for instructions. Of course, all Dryads have their own personalities and the common characteristics of various tree types are listed in the previous chapter. Thus, some Dryads prefer greater freedom to do things their own way, whilst some like to be given precise instructions. But all of them without exception have minds of their own. So a Dryad will not simply do as you tell it to just because you say so. It will consider whether your request conflicts with its own ethical standpoint and matches its skills and it will then act accordingly. It is a partnership that must be worked at and which deepens and improves over time as the two parties – human and Dryad – come to understand and respect each other.

Dusty makes this perfectly clear in the little instructional leaflet that he provides with each LiveWood item. The one which accompanied my own healing wand reads as follows:

> *"Although all the necessary taming rituals have been performed, (in strict accordance with the ancient Woodcraft Lore of the Old Religion), this domesticated Dryad still has a strong personality of Its own.*
>
> *"So beware, you can't make It do anything, and therefore No Guarantee of Its cooperation can be given. If you are wise, you will make friends with It first, before requesting Its help. The more you win Its confidence, and goodwill, the more help it will give you.*

Wyrdwood: The Story of Dusty Miller

> *"Treat It as a personal friend; with tender loving care, consideration and above all, respect; and It will give you a lifetime of devoted service in return. All you need to do, is talk to It to get results!"*

I have mentioned several times that Dusty claims that his family is – to the best of his knowledge, and that of the Dryads with whom he works – the sole source of LiveWood in the world today. It has no doubt occurred to some enterprising minds to questions why this should be the case, and whether it would be possible for them to start making their own LiveWood items? In order to place the situation in context, we need to explore closely the precise nature of the covenant between the Miller Clan and the Dryads.

The first thing that has to be borne in mind is that Dusty is the hereditary Shaman of his tribe. As such, he comes from a family line that has been talking with particular trees for very many generations. This has served to build up a considerable level of trust. This is important because it must never be forgotten that every piece of LiveWood is a living being, the earthly body of a Dryad. The Dryads are as concerned about their personal safety as any human being and they will not entrust just anybody to carve them, shape them and be responsible for their wellbeing. It literally takes generations of human lifetimes to build up this level of trust, but without it the Dryads are not going to offer up LiveWood to anyone, they simply will not entertain the idea.

You may learn to speak with trees and you may succeed in building up a friendship with Dryads, but you will not in your lifetime ever establish the depth of trust and the profundity of mutual understanding that will ever convince them to supply you with LiveWood. Now it's possible that if your descendants continue building on any rapport you establish that maybe in a few generations or so, the Dryads may be willing to supply LiveWood to a member of your future family. Indeed, it would be desirable for this to happen here and there, for Dusty 13th and Dusty 14th are both aware of the fragility of this knowledge and skill being tied to a single family line. One of the primary purposes of this book is to preserve this valuable knowledge. But for others to take up the work too is the work not of years, but of generations, so it is important that people start laying the foundations for that future now.

I am sure there are people reading this who will be thinking, "But why can't I do this now? I'm trustworthy, I can be relied upon." Well, that may be so, but the provision of LiveWood is a calculated risk by the Dryads and the trees simply will not do it without the development of generations of trust.

Dusty and Friend

Wyrdwood: The Story of Dusty Miller

There is another factor which should be mentioned here in order to put the whole matter in clear focus. As part of Dusty's initiation, he had to go to each of the groups of trees with which his family works and deposit a small amount of his blood with them. This gives them a direct link to him, so that they can hold him accountable for the work that he does. In brief, if Dusty does not do what he's supposed to, or mistreats the LiveWood, the trees are able to kill him. That stark fact is a measure of the responsibility involved in his work.

Dusty's task is to collect the LiveWood when he is told to do so. to prepare it for use, and then to allow his hands and tools to be guided as he shapes it into a suitable vehicle for the Dryad who dwells within it, allowing that tree spirit to do its job properly.

Once the piece is complete and has been sold to its new owner, Dusty is no longer responsible for it. Someone might ask what would happen if the purchaser was to misuse or mistreat the finished tool. Well, they must take responsibility for their own actions. A Dryad is perfectly capable of dealing with mistreatment or misappropriation, as was described earlier when I related the tale of the stolen walking stick and how it found its way back to its true owner.

The fact remains, though, that in practice the ultimate human companion to a Dryad seems to be, at least in part, pre-determined, with branches grown for specific purposes, meeting the needs of specific people, before those people have even been born. Dusty is so familiar with the phenomenon of somebody looking over his stock and finding a wand or other item that they 'recognise'. Perhaps they had imagined something of that very shape on their way to see him; perhaps they feel a physical bond when they touch the item, as I did; perhaps it exerts a pull upon their consciousness which they simply cannot ignore. But whatever the case may be, the pairing of human and Dryad seems almost foolproof. Also, the prices for LiveWood reflect the value of the material and what

Wyrdwood: The Story of Dusty Miller

it can do; it is a living thing and will provide a lifetime of service and is thus not 'cheap'. This too makes it unlikely to be purchased on a whim by the feckless. The safeguards seem fairly sure.

Wyrdwood: The Story of Dusty Miller

CHAPTER FIVE

MAGICK BONES AND RUNESCRIPTS

I have an intimate familiarity with runes and a passionate interest in them, and when I was first shown examples of Dusty's LiveWood products, I was immediately attracted to the line of runic lettering that ran along the 'blade' of a little knife shaped from a piece of wood. These runes were tiny and intricate, beautifully written by a craftsman. I could read some of them, as they were evidently very closely related to the Old English *Futhork*, which had been introduced to England by the Anglo-Saxon settlers who arrived after the Romans had departed these shores. But I found it very curious, as there were characters which were subtly different and one or two which I didn't know.

I am very familiar with the variations in the runic characters in different times and places, having studied the subject closely, but I found myself looking at a puzzle. Here were runes which were very obviously derived from the Anglo-Saxon rune row, but there were subtle differences – and even a couple of new characters – which didn't match the variants I had previously seen. There was a story here and I was eager to discover what it was.

Before I travelled to Kent to meet Dusty for the first

time, I did some research to prepare myself. I watched a DVD of one of his talks (see the 'Further Reading' section for details of this) and I read a lot of the material which is available online. It was here that I found the design of a runescript entitled 'To Keep You Safe'. The basic image of the runic design is reproduced below, but this is simply a picture on the page of this book; it is inactive. However, a properly activated copy of this runescript can be found at the website mentioned below, so that you can easily look at the activated rune on your computer screen and print out a copy for your own use when prompted to do so (the web page will automatically prompt you to print it). This particular runescript is provided free for all to use, as Dusty firmly believes that everyone should have it in order to avoid accident or violence in a world that can too often be dangerous.

This runescript was actually made for Dusty himself in 1956 by his father, Dusty Miller 12th. It was intended to keep Dusty safe whilst he was on military service, and it proved to quite literally be a life-saver.

Dusty wore this rune on his dog-tag when he was on active service in Cyprus and he says that it saved him from the 'bullet with his name on it'. Right at the moment that the shot was fired, some impulse prompted Dusty to suddenly turn. This meant that the bullet hit the muscle of his thigh instead of his vitals and he only suffered a flesh wound.

Since that time, many other soldiers have carried this runescript with them into danger, with excellent results. It has accompanied soldiers in Northern Ireland, Israel, the Falklands, the Gulf, the warring states of the old Yugoslavia, Afghanistan and Iraq.

Dusty's runes work on the principle that once activated, they send a subtle visual message directly to your brain, which causes a particular type of response within your subconscious, causing it to wake up and act upon the message received. In the case of this 'To Keep You Safe' runescript, that message directs the subconscious to extend its awareness of danger and act as a kind of 'Guardian Angel', warning you of approaching peril and directing you to avoid it.

The runescript should be printed from the website, carefully cut out and then stuck up somewhere where you will see it often. In this way, it will regularly renew its message, flashing it into your subconscious every time the script catches your eye.

A good idea is to stick the rune on or near the headboard of your bed, so that you see it last thing at night and first thing in the morning. At these times, as you slip from the waking state to sleeping, then back again, it can most easily influence your subconscious.

Dusty's runescripts are powerful transformative tools that can turn people's lives around. But despite its enormous value, there is no charge for this particular runescript, as Dusty believes that everybody deserves to be freely kept safe from accident or the threat of violence. If you have friends or family who you would also like to protect with this powerful rune, they too can obtain their free copies by going to the following website and printing the page when prompted to do so. A runescript obtained in such a manner will come appropriately charged and ready to use. The website address is:
http://www.dustys-lebensholz.de/RuneScript.html

When I met Dusty we spent a little time sharing our perspectives on the runes and he told me the tale of how his ancestors acquired the knowledge of the runes, some 1,500 years ago, back in the period of British history known as the

Wyrdwood: The Story of Dusty Miller

Dark Ages.

> **Dusty Miller**
> Of http://curious-ideas.blogspot.com/
> Wishes You More
> **Success In Life**
> Just LOOK at this Magickal RuneScript often, to retrain your sub-conscious mind for Success in Life!
> www.runescriptsthatwork.com

At that time, Britain was divided into many small rival kingdoms. When we think of kingdoms today, we tend to imagine an entire country united under a single sovereign, but that certainly wasn't the case back then. A kingdom could be a single valley and its occupants, providing the ruling warlord of that valley had sufficient charisma and force of arms to hold onto it.

There were frequent conflicts, as these petty kings sought to enlarge their own rule at the expense of their neighbours'. One king in particular was ambitious and had visions of the whole land unified under his rule. His name was

Wyrdwood: The Story of Dusty Miller

Vortigern and he knew that if he was to stand any hope of success, he would have to bolster his armies with outside help. To this end, he brought in a large number of Germanic mercenaries, led by the Jute warlord brothers Hengist and Horsa.

To cut a long story short, Vortigern's guile led him to some early success, but he ultimately met with a sticky end. But the mercenaries had ambitions of their own and they liked this land they had come to. So Hengist established his own kingdom, setting himself up as a king, with Maidstone as his base of operations. Kent, of course, was the home territory of Dusty's tribe.

Tales began to circulate that the secret of Hengist's success was due to a 'magick bone' that was in his possession and this was something that fascinated the Elves and they determined to learn its secrets.

By devious means, they managed to 'borrow' the magick bone from Hengist's quarters, make a copy of it for their own use, then sneak it back again without him having realised it had been taken. It was quite literally a human thigh bone, upon which the runic alphabet had been inscribed.

Hengist and his henchmen had no idea how the magick operated. They were familiar with the concept of runes, of course, and they knew that the carved letters upon the bone signified powerful magick, but they were not runemasters themselves and had no idea how it worked, nor could they read the letters. They simply trusted that it was a status symbol that brought them genuine success.

The Elves were as unable to read as Hengist and his men, and thus the use of the runes as an alphabet was lost on them. But they had one major advantage in that magick was their stock-in-trade and they understood how to approach the runic mysteries and gradually decode them. This they proceeded to do over the following generations.

One of the things that they discovered was the very real

effect that just seeing a rune would have on the subconscious mind of an observer. Whenever the eye sees a runic shape, it triggers a reaction in the synapses of the brain, which causes a particular chain of thoughts to start running below the threshold of conscious awareness. To put it in a nutshell, every time you look at a rune, you effect a small change in your thinking and perception.

Elfin Runes

Wyrdwood: The Story of Dusty Miller

The effect is a cumulative one, which is why Dusty recommends sticking the 'Keep You Safe' runescript in a place where your eyes will pass over it regularly, reinforcing the positive message within your subconscious. He describes this effect as doing for your right brain processes what the practice of Positive Affirmation does for your left brain.

Over the years, it was observed by the Elves that certain runes had certain effects and they were able to codify the runes according to the message or impulse each one implanted in the subconscious. But they would also occasionally discover – either by intuition or revelation – a new rune, with a new meaning, which they would add to the alphabet. This explains the differences between Dusty's runes, which have evolved organically with his family history, and the Old English *Futhork*, which would undoubtedly have represented the runes as carved on Hengist's 'magick bone'.

In modern times, with increased literacy and availability of source materials, a lot of books about runes have been published, some popular and some scholarly, with the most useful falling somewhere in between. This has made it easier to determine the meanings of runes. But Dusty still uses the tried and tested attributions discovered by his ancestors through the simple and practical method of putting the runes to the test to see what happened. It has also been possible to discover the sound values of the runic alphabet, and to intuitively assign sounds to the newer, purely Elfin, runes. For example, Dusty explained to me that he has five separate runes signifying the sound of the letter 'A'; the one actually chosen for use within a runescript will vary depending upon the meaning of that script. The actual table of runes used by Dusty is illustrated in this chapter.

In classical runework, as practised by those working within the heathen traditions of Northern Europe today, each rune has its meaning and the runemaster will select those runes which best convey the purpose he wishes to achieve. He will then carve or write those runes, often singing their sound values as he does so, or reciting one of the traditional rune poems pertinent to each character. The actual arrangement of the runes may vary considerably. There are examples where the runes simply spell out a message of affirmation; sometimes the numeric value of the runes is symbolically important and two or more runes may be fused into a composite figure. For the creation of talismans, a whole series of runes may be bonded together, forged into a single composite figure that contains all of their shapes; this is termed a 'bind-rune'. Some of the most complex examples of these, known as 'Helms of Awe' (a name taken from the myth of Sigurd and the dragon Fafnir in Norse mythology), can be found in the old Icelandic books of magic, such as the *Galdrabok*, or in my own book *Ægishjálmur*. So there were many and varied ways in which the ingenuity of the runemaster could arrange his runes for maximum effect, giving them a mysterious and evocative appearance in order to captivate the subconscious mind when they caught the eye. The runes would then be 'activated' so that they could carry out their work, a subject we will return to later in the chapter.

The runes were often used in association with traditional formulas, which would be inscribed in runic characters. As an example, one such formula was the word ALU, signifying 'ale'. The runes for A, L and U respectively meant divine inspiration, the passage through life's journey and Earth energy and vitality. So the overall meaning is one of the person's life being enriched and enhanced by streams of inspirational energy from both above and below, from the heavens and the earth. This ecstatic state of being was likened to the uninhibiting, liberating effects of the alcohol in the ale, which was considered to be sacramental.

The way that Dusty uses runes, as discovered by his ancestors and passed down the family line, shares many of the above principles and yet is also very unique and individual.

Wyrdwood: The Story of Dusty Miller

The underlying principles are similar enough to affirm the authenticity of the tradition, yet unique enough to display a knowledge and understanding of runes and their properties which was developed in isolation from the Norse runic tradition, along empirical lines. The important thing to bear in mind is that Dusty's runes get reliable results!

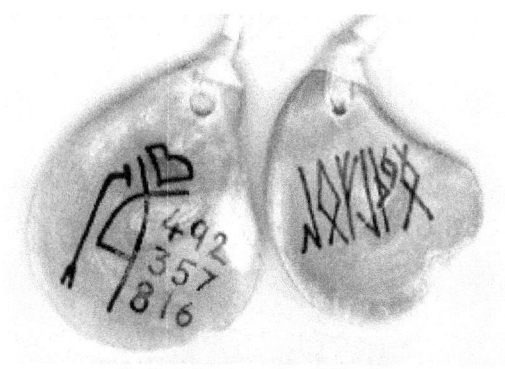

Folk Magick SpellShells

     Dusty does not use the traditional formulas such as ALU, which was described above, because these were not known to his ancestors. Instead, he creates formulae of his own. He will devise a key phrase expressing what he wishes the runes to accomplish, then he will write out that phrase in runic characters. Where there are multiple examples of a given sound value (such as the five instances of the 'A' sound, as mentioned earlier), he will select the rune whose meaning best suits the purpose of the script.

     Once this phrase has been written down, he may rearrange the order of the letters, making some characters larger and others smaller, so that they stand in a pleasing arrangement with each other, their position and proportions assuming a significance.

     Dusty then embellishes the script further by adding

Wyrdwood: The Story of Dusty Miller

other signs, symbols and sigils which are suggestive of the meaning he wishes the runescript to convey, all of which are designed to provoke a response within the subconscious of the person who sees the script.

Evidently, these runescripts of Dusty's fulfill an identical function to the 'Helm' designs and bind-runes that are found in the annals of Norse magick. There are also obvious similarities with the long and intricate engravings of series of runes, often with pictorial supplements such as ships and dragons, which decorate the more ornate runic marker stones in Nordic countries.

So Dusty's runes bear all of the hallmarks of the

traditions of Northern Europe, but they are applied and scripted in a unique way. Although the similarities are clear to see, I have never encountered any other use of runes which are quite the same as Dusty's runescripts. He showed me several designs that have been developed over the years for a multitude of purposes and they are all highly evocative and pleasing to the eye (this latter may seem a trivial point, but it is actually of vital importance when trying to communicate the runes' message to the subconscious of the observer). I found these scripts highly inspirational and have resolved to try my hand at applying my own runic knowledge in a similar fashion in future.

Wyrdwood: The Story of Dusty Miller

    Once a runescript is complete, it is certainly an appealing and eye-catching design, but it is only able to accomplish its purpose and carry out the functions it was created for after certain key runes in the design have been **activated**. This activation is the act of real magick which transforms a pretty picture into an agent capable of causing real change to occur. As such, it is something which is done by someone who has spent years learning the lore of the runes and the necessary checks and balances to ensure their work is correct. In this regard, Dusty says that his dad, Dusty 12th, once told him, "We have to do it Right, as we are always in the eye of our Deities, and can't afford to make mistakes!"

So the key runes are activated to produce their magical effect, and this is enhanced by the effect of the overall design of the script as it is perceived by the subconscious mind; a perfect blend of magic and artistry to create the desired result.

One or two examples of runescript designs are included in this chapter, though you should be aware that these are not 'activated'; if you would like a properly charged runescript, please contact Dusty via the website addresses given in the 'Further Reading' section.

The time was that a runescript had to be activated by a Runemaster at the time it was written down, and then presented to the person it was intended for. But Dusty 13th and Dusty 14th have fully embraced modern technology in their work and have developed a kind of 'quantum physics method', whereby they can display a runescript on a computer screen and switch on the key runes by using the backlight of the screen as part of the process. This electronic runescript will then be fully activated whenever the recipient looks at it.

Once the runescript has been activated by looking at it on screen, you can print out a copy of it on paper, which will work for you because the runescript has been activated for you and the same electronic rune is imprinted on the paper as was displayed on the screen.

However, if you were then to photocopy or copy out by hand the runescript from the printed paper, the copy would simply be a pattern on a piece of paper, inert and unactivated, because it would lack the connection to the initially activated electronic runescript which was triggered in the observer's mind.

It is for this reason that I have referred readers to Dusty's web page about runes, so that you may view and print out a properly activated copy of the runescript 'To Keep You Safe'. The one printed in the pages of this chapter looks the part, but regrettably it is not possible to place an activated runescript within the book.

Wyrdwood: The Story of Dusty Miller

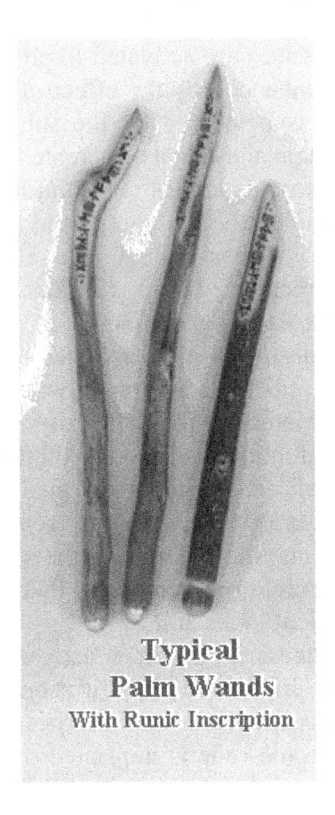

Typical Palm Wands
With Runic Inscription

    As an important and reasonable safeguard, Dusty has ensured that his copyright statement forms an integral part of the design of each of his runescripts and is keyed into the activation process. So removing the copyright declaration will deactivate and nullify the script altogether.

Wyrdwood: The Story of Dusty Miller

CHAPTER SIX

THE OLD RELIGION

Dusty often gets asked whether he is a Witch. His reply is that he was born into an ancient family of English hereditary Witches and that he therefore has all of that ancestral knowledge stored in the back of his skull. But being a Witch is not as simple as that, Dusty has also been through the required training to carry out his role. As was explained earlier, he was initiated as a Tree Witch, or Wise Man, by his father, Dusty Miller 12th, when he was nine years old and began many years of training and apprenticeship at that point.

In addition to the Elf Magick that was passed down his family line, Dusty came to the attention of a woman from a local Coven of Witches. This led to him being initiated into the Ashdown Coven by its High Priestess, Gladys Langridge. Gladys would later marry Bobbie Clutterbuck and was the High Priestess who would ultimately initiate Gerald Gardner into the craft, leading to the Gardnerian Wicca of today.

All of this took place when Dusty was a boy, during the Second World War, and led to the working of weather magick related to the D-Day Landings, which was recounted earlier in the book.

Since then, Dusty has tried to live up to his family's

wyrdwood: The Story of Dusty Miller

heritage, fulfilling the role of 'Village Witch' and helping people as best he can. Dusty explains that in the words of his grandparents he is a hereditary Brown Witch, (brown since he works with Nature and the Earth), one who "walks the chalk", referring to the chalk downs of Kent, his ancestral territory.

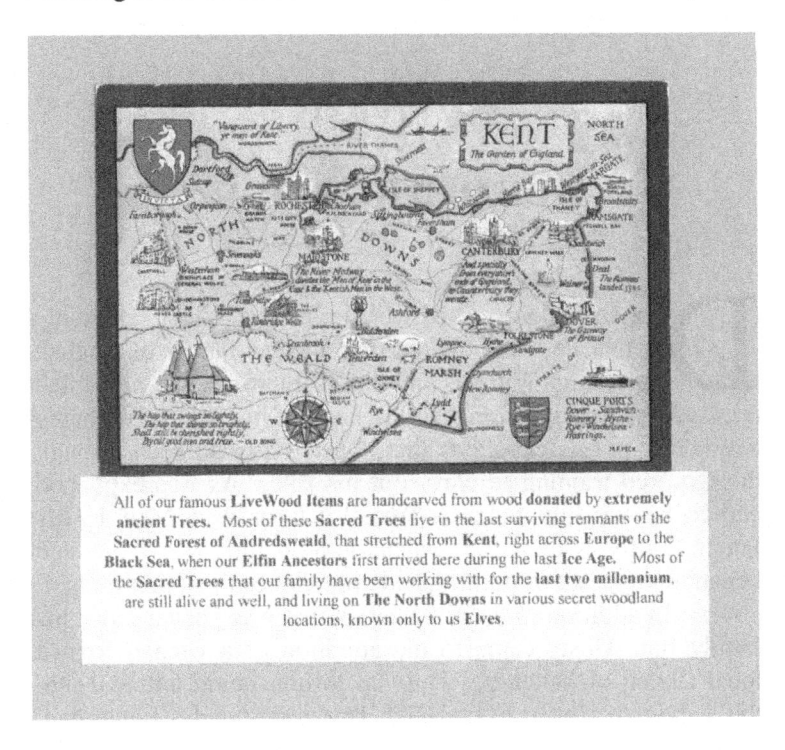

All of our famous **LiveWood Items** are handcarved from wood **donated** by **extremely ancient Trees**. Most of these **Sacred Trees** live in the last surviving remnants of the Sacred Forest of **Andredsweald**, that stretched from **Kent**, right across **Europe** to the **Black Sea**, when our **Elfin Ancestors** first arrived here during the last **Ice Age**. Most of the **Sacred Trees** that our family have been working with for the **last two millennium**, are still alive and well, and living on **The North Downs** in various secret woodland locations, known only to us **Elves**.

Terry Pratchett (a client of Dusty's) has written some great insights about the Witches of the chalk downs in his Tiffany Aching novels (*The Wee Free Men, A Hat Full of Sky, Wintersmith* and *I Shall Wear Midnight*). His books are full of more genuine understanding of true Witchcraft than most titles you will find in the 'occult' section of any bookshop. Dusty declares that Terry has the most comprehensive understanding of Witches and Witchcraft of anyone he has ever met, and this is all fed into his stories, along with a large spoonful of humour.

Dusty recommends reading Terry's stories in order and enjoying the tale, but also read between the lines and discover what is really being said about Witches. Here are gathered all the hidden secrets that you won't find in most books on Witchcraft: why Witches who live on chalk are different from those who live on limestone or rock; why some wear black and some don't; when magick is appropriate and when it is not; why Boffo is never discussed, and so much more. You can learn much from these books and have a good laugh while doing so. They are full of things you need to know and understand which the Witchcraft textbooks don't tell you.

Witchcraft is often called "the Old Religion", indeed Dusty himself calls it by that name in the instructional papers that accompany some of his LiveWood items. Religions invariably involve Gods and Goddesses, so if we are to understand it properly we should acquire a knowledge of these Deities. There were so many Gods and Goddesses with so many names – some of them aspects of the others, or slightly different cultural perceptions of the same Divinity – that the Elves tended to refer to them as "the Folks Upstairs", as we have already established. But there are four main figures who feature large in the religious background of Elfin Magick, and they are as follows:

<u>Sola or Mylord</u>: This is the Elfin name for the Sun, the shining one who guides our Higher Self. He is a God of left brain consciousness, teaching the ways of the intellect and the means of transmitting knowledge through words and definitions.

<u>Luna or Mylady</u>: This is the Elfin name for the Moon, the Goddess who guides our Higher Self. She teaches via right brain consciousness, using the medium of pictures, colours,

sensations and feelings. She guides through intuition.

Jaia or Grandmother: The supreme feminine life force, Mother Nature, the very Earth on which we stand. She is the Mother of all and a Goddess of wisdom who teaches what we need to know through the old brain functions of the harmonised tricameral mind. The Elfin name uses the soft 'J' initial sound instead of the harder 'Gaia' found in other sources.

Aether or Grandfather: The supreme masculine life force, the sky above, the air surrounding us, the very life-sustaining atmosphere of the planet. Aether is a strange and silent God, who pays little personal attention to us, but nevertheless provides every one of us with the means to live and breathe.

One important feature of Dusty's work is the way in which he uses Leylines. These are lines of Earth energy which criss cross the entire surface of the planet. Their course is often marked by ancient monuments and they can be traced on the landscape (by those unable to directly sense their power) by connecting ancient sites on the map, where several of these places will seem to form a straight line, often running for many miles. Leylines are similar to the energy meridians of the human body which are used and stimulated in acupuncture, but these are the energy meridians of the planet itself, carrying currents of Earth power. Although they have become known as Leylines in recent years, since Alfred Watkins brought them to wider notice, the Elfin name for them is simply Powerlines, since they were a powerful energy source for their magical work.

Wherever two or more Leylines cross, a power vortex is formed, where the energy is multiplied and the veil between worlds is very thin. The more lines that cross at a point, the more powerful the vortex and the greater the effect. Dusty's home is built upon such a vortex and he has skillfully directed the energies to encompass the house and to flow through it in specific ways, greatly assisting in his work.

Even people who are not attuned to Ley energy will notice its effects, feeling a sense of comfort and peace when they stand in the current. Dusty remarks that although four leaf clovers can be found anywhere, they are rare in most places. However, 90% of four leaf clovers occur on Leylines. To prove the point, he went out in 1984 to see how many he could discover and he found 932 four-leaf, 311 five-leaf and 6 six-leaf clovers, all on Leylines, showing conclusively how easy they are to find there.

The Dryads of trees growing in areas charged with Ley energy (such as Dusty's area of Kent) also seem to be much more approachable and keener to work with humans, as if the Leys energise and enthuse them just as they do us.

Trees are very responsive to Ley energy in general and it is quite common for trees on Leylines to develop multiple trunks. That is to say, they will possess a normal root system but will have two or three trunks. Trees growing where Leylines cross may have four or more trunks and this increases with the number of lines crossing. The biggest cluster that Dusty knows of is seventeen trunks belonging to an ancient 'Grandmother' beech tree.

One of the most useful things about Leycrosses, where Leylines meet, is that they provide doorways to other worlds. The veil between this world and other dimensional existences is very thin at such places, and although the body is firmly rooted in our own reality, the mind is not so constrained and it can reach through these doorways and experience other ways of being. This makes Leycrosses perfect places to meditate, talk to tree spirits or engage in other kinds of psychic research.

Dusty's homes have always been chosen at Leycross sites, so that he can take advantage of their huge supply of energy and psychic activity to assist in his work.

It is important to point out that Ley energy is

Wyrdwood: The Story of Dusty Miller

inexorable and gives no thought to anyone who gets in its way, so it has to be handled and channeled with great care. In particular, the flow of Earth energy often leads to the generation of strong winds and storm currents that blow along Leylines. Electrical storms, thunder and lightning, are also more frequent in areas with a large density of Leylines.

This Sacred DURMAST OAK (Wintereik) has seven trunks with a meditation space in the centre of them. This is because it has been growing in a Ley-Vortex for over 1,700 years. This means it was old when Mohammed was born.

My family have been meditating here for many centuries and as you can see, we continue to do so. This tree also supplies us with LiveWood for our very effective Healing Tools.

When describing himself, Dusty uses the word 'Shaman'. So it's appropriate to spend a little time examining this word to find out exactly what he means by it.

Basically, a Shaman is the member of a tribe who is responsible for all magical operations and for contacting other worlds on behalf of the tribespeople. It is the Shaman who is able to intuit and interpret the instructions from the tribal Deities and communicates these to the members of the tribe. He (or she) also assists individual tribe members to balance and harmonise the different parts of their own minds, allowing the tribe as a whole to remain attuned to their ancestors and Deities.

The position of Shaman is usually an inherited one, passing the skills on from one generation to the next and also keeping available access to a Family Memory, where the current Shaman can find the wisdom and insight of those who have gone before made available to him.

Dusty recalls an old saying: "It doesn't matter if a Shaman is a man, or a woman, or both, as long as they can ride the Sha!" The 'Sha' is the name of the principal energy used, and is of a similar nature to the 'Chi', 'Ki', 'Prana' and so forth named by other traditions. It is an immensely powerful energy and can be felt most strongly in the LiveWood artifacts that Dusty makes. This energy is particularly strong and accessible to Dusty in the 'eerie eyrie' level of his house, where the Ley energy is channeled to create what he describes as his "Quantum Consciousness Communications Centre".

In order to describe the process of human consciousness as it interacts with other worlds via the Higher Self, Dusty reaches a stumbling block. There are any number of good words to describe various things and states of being which are used among the occult community today. The big problem is, that everyone who uses these words tends to mean something slightly different from everyone else, so the picture very quickly becomes confused. So Dusty cannot use those words, because you may then assume you know what he's talking about when you don't, because your interpretation of the words may differ to his.

So Dusty prefers to do things the old-fashioned way and teach his ideas in the way his Elfin grandfather used to teach him, back in the days when these words were simply not in broad circulation. Instead, they had to rely on metaphor to get the right message across. So that is what will be used here, the Elfin metaphor of 'The Horse and Rider', to explain the process of magical consciousness.

"The Horse with an Invisible Rider"

© TDM 2007

An Elfin Metaphor

Dusty explains that there is an invisible, psychic world which is all around us all the time. It has always been there and it has always been known to be there, but most people choose to ignore it or pretend it doesn't exist, because they cannot see it with their physical eyes.

We can see a good illustration of this kind of skewed perspective in modern science. You will hear scientists telling you that our planet exists in a universe that is full of stars. But a competent astronomer will tell you that a mere 5% of the substance of the universe is composed of stars and star systems. The remaining volume is 25% Dark Matter and 70% Dark Energy. But because these cannot be seen, they are ignored. Only the stars are seen, so only the stars get talked about. The unseen (but much larger) remainder is considered a weird subject to be studied by weird people. It's actually uncomfortable for most people to try to think about the invisible universe, so they don't try. Instead, they choose to be economical with the truth, talking only about the things that can be seen.

The simple metaphor taught by Dusty's grandfather to explain human experience of the visible and invisible worlds goes as follows. First, you should imagine yourself to be a horse (be good to yourself, of course, picture yourself to be the handsomest, most beautiful and majestic horse you can imagine).

The horse has a rider upon its back, however, and that rider is invisible. Because the horse has eyes that can see forwards or sideways, but not backwards, it can never see the rider upon its back. And because the rider is invisible, no other horse can see it either.

Now let's picture you – the horse – going steadily down the road, when you start to fancy a cup of tea. There is a café around the corner and you turn and look at it longingly, preparing to go over to it. But the rider has other ideas and uses the reins to steer you back in the direction you were going. In such a case, we might say that you were acting on a 'hunch', as some guidance had come out of seemingly nowhere, prompting you to follow a certain course of action which may not be what you were originally intending.

Sometimes, if the horse has been responding to direction particularly well, the rider might lean forward and whisper some words of encouragement in the horse's ear. Sometimes, the horse will react by jumping about the place and declaring loudly to all and sundry that it has heard the word of God, perhaps setting up a new religion in consequence. This

Wyrdwood: The Story of Dusty Miller

probably isn't quite the reaction (or over-reaction, rather) the rider would have been hoping for, but it does sometimes happen. But this is also the kind of experience that will – more positively – turn a sensitive into a Shaman, or a believer into a saint.

There remains a problem, of course, in that the horse and rider do not speak the same language. Some horses block out the rider's words, insisting they are hallucinatory, declaring that this invisible being cannot exist because they cannot see it. Others may hear the rider's words too often but not be able to fathom their meaning, becoming schizophrenic. But some will work hard to understand what the rider wants, building a common language. Horse and rider will then move in unison, outpacing other horses and accomplishing feats that their fellows can scarcely believe.

This little metaphor makes clear the relationship between a person's ordinary physical personality and their Higher Self; also between the physical world and other-dimensional places. You can now use your own preferred labels for these things, but we'll all understand what exactly we mean.

Now that we have an image in our minds of the relationship between worlds and between the Higher Self and ordinary consciousness, we can take a look at how Dusty defines magick. To him, magick is something that works on many levels of consciousness to produce results. People whose eyes and minds are closed to worlds beyond the physical may find this a baffling and inexplicable phenomenon. However, it is entirely natural and comprehensible to those who are aware of higher levels of consciousness and understand how the visible and invisible worlds interknit.

Dusty spells 'magick' the old-fashioned way, with a 'k' at the end, in order to distinguish it from the stagecraft and sleight of hand employed by stage magicians.

Dusty suggests that if you imagine your mind as a

computer, then a magick spell is a specially written software program which will cause certain routines to run and things to happen, which may benefit your body, mind and spirit all at the same time.

Most people who express an interest in things magical or psychic, or who know about such things as Leylines, are also very interested in megalithic stones. There are a number of such ancient monuments in the woods that Dusty frequents. Dusty explains that this local forest does not actually appear to have a name. If you look for it on a map, it's just the bit of old woodland between North Downs Way and the Pilgrims Way. Of course, Dusty's ancestors didn't read or write names on maps anyway. This was a forest which they knew to be full of sacred trees, so to them it was simply known as 'Holy Hill'.

Callenash

Wyrdwood: The Story of Dusty Miller

Hidden away within this forest are numerous megalithic stones, which are known as 'Grey Wethers'. As was mentioned in chapter one, they weren't placed there by Dusty's people, the Elves, but by another aboriginal tribe which Dusty's ancestors called 'The Horned Ones' and who were later termed 'Goblins' by the Celts.

Although the Elfin tribespeople could naturally sense the power flow of the Leylines that ran through the forest, the Horned Ones were not able to do so. When they managed to locate a Leycross, therefore, they would leave these mighty stone markers to mark their position so that they would be able to find them again, and make use of the Earth energies that gathered and flowed in these special places. They were doing this in Dusty's part of Kent, with its great concentration of Leylines, over a thousand years before Stonehenge was constructed.

LeyCross Marker Stone

Most of these stones are hidden away in the forested landscape and are not found on any maps or other reference works, being largely ignored by the 'experts' who are more interested in the more impressive appearing and more famous examples to the west. But those in this little part of Kent are about a thousand years older and and have a more powerful

Wyrdwood: The Story of Dusty Miller

'feel' than their better known brethren, as proven by experience. They are made of a kind of sandstone and usually display strange holes in their surfaces. Dusty loves to lay his hands on these old stones and says that they buzz with energy and are usually warm to the touch. Even in winter, snow that falls on them will melt, leaving the stones looking dry and warm in the middle of a snowy landscape.

As we have discovered, the whole forest is crisscrossed with Leylines and every energy line that flows into the forest, or leaves it, is marked with a megalith, forming a great energy loop about the area. Dusty wonders if one day someone might set about finally mapping all of the stones and discovering the pattern they yield, someone enterprising enough to determine what they mean, how they channel the Ley energy, and why they are arranged as they are.

The Elves referred to these local Sarsen stones, marking the site of Ley-crosses, as 'Singing Stones'. The reason for this is that when they sit upon them to get a 'feel' for the site marked by the stone, they are able to hear what they call 'Faerie Music', a kind of singing which sounds like a Gregorian chant or Plainsong heard at a distance, or through an abbey wall. Dusty suspects this may be a lingering thought-form placed within the stone to guide travellers by the Horned Ones, just as the Elves would leave messages with Sacred Trees for those who might have lost their way.

One of the better known megalithic sites in Dusty's locality is called Coldrum. It was originally a chambered tomb, with earth heaped over it, ringed about with Sarsen stones. But many centuries of erosion have left it a three-sided room, roofless, with a 15 feet (5 metre) drop falling away from it, though the ring of Sarsens is still there. Dusty goes there a lot to honour his ancestors, because in the 1930s twenty-two skeletons were unearthed there, all possessing the bathrocranic skulls peculiar to the Elves (known to modern scientists as the 'Brünn' people). Ordinarily, the Elves would burn their dead

Wyrdwood: The Story of Dusty Miller

and bury the ashes in a basket (which may be the origin of the Christian saying of "going to Hell in a basket"!) It is a mystery why this large group of Elves were buried here in a pile during the Bronze Age; perhaps they fell foul of the Dwarves (Bronze Age copper prospectors). In any case, Dusty goes there quite often and is very familiar with the place.

Dusty relates how on one occasion he took an American visitor to see the site and in the process discovered a very interesting effect of the Coldrum power vortex. The visitor was a cameraman from Burbank Studios in California. He arrived suddenly at Dusty's home, wanting to film an interview with him about his work with LiveWood. But he said that he wanted to film the interview against an authentic "ancient English" background so that he could prove to the folks back home that he'd really been to England to film these "limey weirdoes".

Dusty could sense that this cameraman was very likely to ridicule his beliefs, so he and his son discussed the matter and decided to take the man to Coldrum. They figured that even if the film was less than satisfactory, at least the background would be suitably impressive and thus they might be able to obtain a couple of good publicity stills from it.

So they took their visitor to Coldrum. Because he had so much heavy and expensive photographic equipment in his car, they ignored the official car park and guided him down the farm track that leads directly to the site. The site itself is surrounded by railings to discourage over-enthusiastic visitors who might damage it. There is an area behind the 'room' but still within the Sarsen ring, that is used as a ritual space by the various Pagans and Witches who visit Coldrum, and it was in this spot that the Dustys decided to film the interview.

Dusty adopted a suitably impressive stance, with one foot resting on a large stone near the room area, and waited for the interviewer to set up the camera. This was one of the large, suitcase-sized video cameras of the 1980s, powered by huge, multi-cell batteries. The man got it set up on a tripod and prepared to begin shooting.

No sooner had they started filming the interview than the camera's batteries drained and became flat. The cameraman was nonplussed, but apologised and returned to the car for a replacement. Dusty was in position, so he had to remain still while he waited. But he couldn't help noticing that the ancient beech tree which overlooked the site was quaking with laughter, its leaves rustling despite the total lack of any breeze. Several of the other nearby trees seemed to be sniggering to themselves too. At this point, however, he thought nothing more of it, as Dryads often do find the strange antics of Humans amusing.

The interviewer returned with a replacement battery pack, attached it to his camera set-up, and resumed filming. By the time Dusty reached his third sentence, the cameraman was literally jumping up and down in frustration, as this second battery had also drained away to nothing, with no power left at all. He tramped off to the car for his third and final battery, puzzled and muttering, whilst all around Dusty could see the trees shaking with laughter. He knew for sure now that this was no mere coincidence.

The cameraman returned with his third and final battery pack, but discovered that his tripod had been disturbed by the constant rummaging about as he attached and detached successive batteries. By the time he had straightened and retightened the tripod, the third battery was completely flat.

He flew into a wild rage, stomping about and cursing. Dusty was getting quite concerned, hoping that the man wouldn't believe him to be to blame.

Then the interviewer had a brainwave. In his car he had a straightforward tape recorder and a very expensive, top of the range, Japanese camera that could not possibly let him down. He decided that they would simply record the interview and he would take some high quality photographs to accompany the words. So he returned to his car and came back with the camera and tape recorder.

It will doubtless come as no surprise to learn that both items, sleek and expensive though they were, were battery operated. Both were flat in no time. The interviewer raged and swore, whilst the trees shook with mirth.

Of course, this left them with no choice but to call it a day and return home. The poor old visitor was so wound up and agitated that he wouldn't even accept the invitation of a cup of tea, but tore off back to London with all speed, without his interview.

The two Dustys have returned to Coldrum since and conducted experiments with other batteries, all of which are rapidly drained by some force at the site. Whether the two types of energy are incompatible, or whether the power vortex at the site literally absorbs other energy sources into itself, is unknown. But this failure of, or interference with, electrical equipment has been noted in many other paranormal cases, such as poltergeist activity and UFO sightings. The vortex at Coldrum is an especially powerful one, with no less than seven Leylines running through the site.

Dusty has had quite a bit of experience with megalithic stones, since he uses the Ley energies to enhance his work with the Dryads when creating LiveWood items; the additional energy makes the whole process easier and gives it a real boost. On one occasion, after he had finished his apprenticeship, he moved to a house which had five Leylines crossing through it, and its foundations were also built upon the Sarsen stones of a ruined stone circle which had once marked the position of the Leycross.

A prehistoric grave found in the garden of this house yielded the body of a man who had been buried there 5,600 years earlier. Experts were certain that more bodies would be found there, but Dusty refused to let them dig them up, feeling it better that they should be allowed to rest in peace. Though they were never bothered by the presence of the bodies beneath this house, the power vortex caused by the large Leycross meant that no one in the family could drink alcohol on the premises, as it made them so sensitive that just the tiniest amount would cause the most terrible hangovers.

Dusty has performed rituals at megalithic sites on several occasions and is often delighted to see birds sitting nearby with their heads on one side, watching with interest. At Stonehenge, there are a family of jackdaws who live under one of the stone lintels. Three of them once sat in a row, observing the ritual taking place at the site, and when it had finished they flew off, one of them throwing down a black feather to Dusty in acknowledgement, which he still keeps as a reminder.

On another occasion, at a local Cromlech known as "the Chestnuts", the group decided that it might be a nice idea to show their appreciation to the stones by singing 'tones'. The atmosphere of the place became better and better as they continued, and to their amazement a pair of rabbits came to see what they were up to. Anyone who knows how timid and skittish wild rabbits are will realise how extraordinary an event this was.

The Chestnuts

Wyrdwood: The Story of Dusty Miller

Another of the local standing stones is called "the White Horse Stone", named after the coat of arms of Hengist, the first official King of Kent. It doesn't actually look anything like a horse, of course, although it is about the same size in height, length and width. The White Horse Stone was once what is called a 'Maid Stone' (similar to the one which gave the town of Maidstone in Kent its name). A Maid Stone is one which produces a special kind of energy out of the top of the stone. When a lady who is having trouble conceiving lies on the flat top of a Maid Stone, its energies work upon her, assisting her in moving from being a maid to being a mother, hence the stone's name. Dusty's clients have used it on many occasions with great success.

A 'MaidStone'

Wyrdwood: The Story of Dusty Miller

Dusty offers another little tale which illustrates the way in which magick works. Magick is never a case of a puff of smoke and a zapping noise and everything is changed as you see in movies. It's much more subtle than that. Magick is a product of consciousness, so it begins by changing consciousness, which changes behaviour, which changes action, which changes events, until suddenly, before you know it, your desired result has happened under your very nose. This can be quite startling to begin with, as you often don't even notice the result creeping up on you until it happens, but it can be hard for the mind to pin down the point at which reality changed, it has slipped through so naturally.

Dusty was reminded of this magical technique when he saw a trader counting money at a local market. He could tell from the expression on the man's face that business hadn't been good, as he was scowling, obviously disappointed by the day's takings. The problem is, this attitude and demeanour will not encourage other customers to buy. Who wants to buy from a grumpy trader? So business will remain poor, and may even worsen. There is an old Chinese proverb: **"a man without a smiling face should not open a shop!"**

During the depression of the 1970s, Dusty says that he used to work on the markets in order to feed his family and keep the wolf from the door. Naturally, he used his Elfin Magick to enhance his prospects. He did this by improving his attitude, which led in turn to him increasing his sales. He is willing to share this piece of magical know-how here in order to help those who may find themselves in a similar situation.

Firstly, he would make sure to count the notes **only**, leaving the coins to accumulate in his money belt without interference.

Secondly, having counted the notes, he would fold the wad of notes in half, thereby doubling its thickness. He stresses that you need to do this with real determination, squeezing the wad tightly into a solid lump. This gives your subconscious the visual and tactile message that you have doubled your money.

While you do this, you need to mentally tell yourself, with complete and utter conviction, that you will successfully double your money before you finish trading for the day. You should tense the muscles in both arms as you do so, which signals your intention to both the money you are holding and your own subconscious mind.

In this way, your whole body and mind know that you are going to be so nice and friendly and helpful to prospective customers that they will like you so much that they will want to buy from you.

Dusty used this technique very successfully on numerous occasions. He recalls one occasion in 1983, when he and his son, Dusty 14th, attended a New Age Fair, where they set up a stall with a view to selling some of their magickal items. But the cost of attending this fair had been so high, and business was so slow, that as the day wore on they both became concerned that they might end up making no profit at all.

Dusty did his folding money magick, and just as the fair was drawing to its close and they were beginning to pack their merchandise away ready for the journey home, a fellow in T-shirt and shorts arrived.

The man explained that he was a computer programmer and had been unable to get away from his work to attend the fair any earlier. So the two Dustys got their handcrafted LiveWood products out on display again, and their new customer took a wad of £50 notes out of his pocket (back in those days, £50 was considered a lot of money; it was a week's wage to some people). So the computer programmer got his LiveWood items and Dusty made a good profit from his attendance at the fair after all, thanks to this neat little magical act.

With all of its talk of Leylines, this chapter would not

be complete without a brief mention of the warmly regarded British archaeologist and dowser Tom Lethbridge, and the influence that his ideas have had upon Dusty. I made a passing reference to Lethbridge earlier, when I presented the table which displayed the 'pendulum rates' for various types of tree.

Tom Lethbridge was an archaeologist who studied at Cambridge, and later became the keeper of Anglo-Saxon antiquities at the Archaeological Museum in Cambridge. He wrote several respected books in his field, but retired from Cambridge in 1957, tired of the stuffiness and blinkered attitudes of academia. He settled in Hole House, in Branscombe, Devon, and it was here, in the latter years of his life, that he produced the works for which he is most remembered.

One of Lethbridge's neighbours was a witch and he enjoyed many conversations with her. He learned to discern the supernatural world by means of a pendulum. But he was no ordinary dowser, he was meticulous in his research and he learned that everything has its own rate of vibration, measured by the length of the pendulum cord at which it responds. Moreover, he discovered that thoughts and abstract ideas such as 'redness', 'anger' or 'death' also had their own pendulum rates. He went on to publish several books detailing his research and charting the evolution of his ideas, and he formulated fascinating theories on the nature of hauntings, life energy, life after death, and worlds beyond the physical. Although most of his books are sadly out of print, they remain available from good second hand sources on the internet and are highly recommended.

Dowsing is one excellent way of following and charting the flow of Ley energy, and Dusty has also used Lethbridge's techniques to chart the vibrational rates of various types of tree. The ideas and practices developed by Tom Lethbridge have opened up new and exciting ways to explore the invisible worlds.

Wyrdwood: The Story of Dusty Miller

No overview of the Old Religion as brought down through the centuries by the Elves of Dusty's tribe would be complete without a consideration of the Luna Calendar they use to measure the year. This is a little different from some of the calendars you may have seen in other books on magical matters, as it has been passed down through the generations secretly by word of mouth.

You may wonder why it is necessary to have a Luna Calendar. What is wrong with the calendar that is in general use, measured by the Earth's yearly journey around the Sun? Well, there is nothing wrong with it, it is very useful as far as it goes. But it pays attention to only one, larger cycle and doesn't effectively reflect the other important cycles through the passage of the year. The twelve months as they now exist are completely arbitrary divisions. They have been shifted around so much that they have lost all meaning they may once have had. For example, 'September' means the seventh month, and 'October' means the eighth month, but these are now respectively the ninth and tenth months, so all meaning and sense and order has been lost.

As Dusty explains it, the purpose of the Luna Calendar is to ensure that people can be in the right place, at the right time, to reap the full benefits of the Moon's biological tides and become one with the living planet. In the days when this calendar was formulated, long before the Celts came to Britain, the year was shorter, having 360 days, and even the days were shorter.

The names of the months seem to have originated during prehistoric times, and each month also has a pictorial symbol associated with it, as they were identified long before people learned to write. Each year consisted of thirteen moons (or months), commencing at Yule. But now that the year is longer, each year starts at the first New Moon after Yule, and may have twelve or thirteen months. Technically, each year contains twelve and one third months, but in practice the Elves have two years of twelve months each, followed by a third year with thirteen months. (Other pagan calendars which have been revived in the modern day make different arrangements and calculations to achieve a similar result.)

The thirteen moons are as follows, in their proper order:

Snow Moon

As the first moon after Yule, this is named for obvious reasons.

Death Moon

This moon is named because of the intense cold of this time of year, when food is scarce and hypothermia is a real danger. The most dangerous moon for the weak and needy.

Awakening Moon

Spring is around the corner. Days are perceptibly that little bit longer and that little bit warmer.

Wyrdwood: The Story of Dusty Miller

Grass Moon
Spring arrives properly, grass and fodder for cattle begins to grow again.

Planting Moon
The soil is now soft enough and the days warm enough to allow the planting of crops and foodstuffs to take place.

Rose Moon
This name is self-explanatory as flowers are in abundance. Dusty suggests that the name may once have simply been 'Flower Moon', with the particular symbol of the rose being adopted when the moon names were later standardised.

Lightning Moon
Thunder and lightning are always at their worst and are most

common during the seventh month, when summer storms clear the mugginess from the air.

Harvest Moon
The time for gathering in the harvest and storing it in preparation for winter.

Hunter's Moon
This is the time for stocking up the meat larder, for deciding which of the livestock will survive the winter and which should be eaten.

Falling Leaf Moon
Autumn has arrived and the leaves are falling from the trees. These would be gathered up by the Elfin tribespeople to provide insulation against the coming cold.

Wyrdwood: The Story of Dusty Miller

Tree Moon
This is the time for cutting wood for winter fuel, or transplanting trees.

Long Night Moon
The name of this moon is very apt, as winter deepens and the shortest day of the year is at hand.

Ice Moon
Due to a shift in the Earth's axis, this thirteenth moon, the Ice Moon, now only occurs every third year, as a kind of 'leap moon'. Its name is self-explanatory, the coldest time of the year, the big freeze.

Each month, at the time of the Full Moon, the local priestess would honour the Goddess with one of the monthly **Esbat Festivals**, at the time when the Goddess Luna was most visible and Her power was at its peak. The Elves were fully aware of the subtle influences the phases of the Moon had upon them, and upon every other living thing.

The Full Moon meetings, known as Esbats, are named

Wyrdwood: The Story of Dusty Miller

after the sacred Tree Spirits presiding over the site at which each Esbat was held. These Esbat sites are always located at Leycrosses, where the Leyline energies are amplified into a power vortex. Their names and residing Tree Spirits are as follows for each moon respectively:

1. Ashgrove
2. Aldergrove
3. Willow
4. Whitethorn
5. Oakgrove
6. Hollytree
7. Hazel
8. Appletree
9. Blackthorn
10. Eldertree
11. Yewtree
12. Birchgrove
13. Rowantree

So each month in the Luna Calendar has a name and a symbol and also a presiding Dryad which watches over it from the site at which its Esbat is performed. These thirteen trees are not the only ones considered sacred to the Elves, but these are deemed to be the original thirteen Holy Trees.

The New Year begins at Yule, the turning of the year. This is a precise date which is easily determined by observation. If you watch the sunrise each day from autumn, you will notice that it moves slightly to the right from its previous position each day. But at the winter solstice, the direction reverses and it begins to slowly creep back left again. Because the day has already begun when you first notice this, the following day is actually counted as the first day of Yule and the beginning of the New Year.

The Yuletide Festival lasts for twelve days, until Holy

Wyrdwood: The Story of Dusty Miller

Thorn Day. At this time, Holy Trees all over the country burst into flower. The most well known of these is the Glastonbury Holy Thorn, but there are many of them all over the country and if you look, you will be sure to find one not too far from you.

If you wish to celebrate the Esbats, you will need to find a group of the appropriate kind of tree in your area, with a Leyline (or preferably a Leycross) running through it, and make friends with the Dryad there. You can then devise a simple rite that feels intuitively right to you to call upon Luna with the assistance of the Dryad.

There are other special festivals throughout the year, relating to the four Elements. Because these festivals are Sun-related rather than Moon-related, they occur on the same dates each year in the conventional Solar calendar:

March 25th – **Ladyday**

This is the Festival of Earth, when honour is given to the Earth Mother and the Spirits of the Land. This was the original Mother's Day celebration.

July 15th – **Well Blessing Day**

This day is the Festival of Water, hence the ritual act of blessing the well. Thanks are given to the Goddess for the waters. When Christianity pervaded society, changing the old festivals and giving them new names, they named this St Swithin's Day, with the notion attached that if it rained on this day then it would continue raining for forty days and forty nights, so the original meaning of the day is still discernible.

September 29th – **Michaelmas**

This Festival of Air marks the end of the growing season. It is a time for giving thanks for the harvest and for asking for assistance with the hunting season, so that enough food may be gathered in for the winter.

December 24th – **Yuletide Tree Festival**
Yuletide is the Festival of Fire, when Mother Earth and the Dryads are thanked for all of their help and assistance, and for providing deadwood as fuel for fires in the cold season.

The four **Sabbats** are well known in occult circles. They are four Solar festivals which fall at the midpoints between the solstices and equinoxes.

These Sabbats were originally festivals of Fire and Air, used to celebrate the beneficence of Jaia and Aetha, Mother Earth and Father Sky. They were intended to bless and sanctify the union of Earth and Sky, so that the Sky would continue to fertilise the Earth, bringing forth abundance. The Sabbats were originally named after the presiding Wind Deities, but they have now been renamed and rejigged and their original meaning has been lost. They are still a good occasion for thanksgiving and celebration if approached in the right spirit, though.

The Luna Calendar was devised in a time when the cycles of nature were more interwoven with our everyday lives, a time when the new day was sensibly presumed to begin when the Sun rose over the horizon instead of beginning at an arbitrary hour on the clock in the middle of the night. It is a very organic and meaningful calendar, that is reminiscent of life being lived according to its proper rhythms. This is something we suffer from having lost touch with in this day and age, something which we would benefit from returning to.

Wyrdwood: The Story of Dusty Miller

Wyrdwood: The Story of Dusty Miller

CHAPTER SEVEN

LITTLE KNOWN WORDS FROM OUR PAGAN PAST

Dusty maintained a very interesting blog on MySpace which detailed many of his interests, beliefs and outlooks, providing a valuable window upon his work. Much of this material has been absorbed into this book and preserved for posterity. One of the really interesting series of postings he used to make concerned old-fashioned words which were pertinent to his work and location. These were words which had been common in his father's day, but which are falling out of favour in the modern world and sadly being lost from us. Words and that which they express are important, they shape the way we think, the way we look at the world (George Orwell's *Nineteen-Eighty-Four* had a lot to say about this). So I am pleased to present the cream of Dusty's discussions of these fine old words here in this chapter. See if you can start slipping one or two of them back into your daily speech.

The Dusty Millers are the descendants of a tribe who have always lived in **'The High Weald of Kent and Sussex'**, which makes them **'Wealdenfolc'**, or 'Wild Woodfolk'.

The **'Weald'** of Kent and Sussex was originally called

Wyrdwood: The Story of Dusty Miller

'**Andredsweald**', the Home of the Goddess. The Dwarfish invaders who arrived in the Bronze Age named it after **Andred**, their Earth Mother Goddess. Of course, Dusty's people had been living there for long ages before that, but they didn't tend to give things such specific names, they simply called them for what they were. So to them, the Weald was their **Wildwood Homelands**.

Looking down onto the mist-filled Weald

Later, in the Iron Age, following the coming of the Celts to Britain, they named their Mother Goddess **Tann**, which transformed into **Saint Anne** as Britain was Christianised and old pagan places and names were absorbed into the new religion.

Weald is a word which means a natural, self-seeded forest, one which is so old that it was here long before mankind began poking around in it. It may be referred to as the **WildWood**, the **GreenWood**, or even the **TangleWood** due to its thick undergrowth and lack of paths.

The Weald was the home of the Elfin tribes, who were

forced to live deep within the woods, out of sight of the Celtic invaders. In later times, when they used to attack intruders and travellers in the forest as revenge, this led to the Celts creating the saying which is still well known today: "When in the woods, whatever you do, don't leave the path!"

England has known several waves of invading settlers, and after the Celts came the Anglo-Saxons, who divided the land into Counties. The Weald became part of three different Counties (which were known in later Saxon times as the **'Holme Counties'**). **Kent** was 'Over-the-Hills' to the North and East; **Sussex** was 'Over-the-Hills' to the South and West; and **Surrey** was in the North-West. The actual Weald had by now been denuded of half its trees and had taken on a rural garden aspect, becoming known as **'Holmesdale'**.

The hills forming the northern and southern boundaries of the Weald are known as the **North and South Downs**. Their crests or tops are called **'headlands'**, their slopes are called **'hills'** and the valleys between them are called **'bottoms'**. These seem like good, sensible names, but it is unknown where the name **Downs** itself came from; perhaps it is an example of English humour?

Most of the people who then lived in Kent, Surrey and Sussex considered themselves very sophisticated. Except, of course, for the **'Wild Folk'** living deep within the forest of Holmesdale.

The remnants of the ancient forest which had once covered the entire land were referred to as the **'Wild'** and its inhabitants were known as **'Wildmen'**, **'Wealdenmen'**, **'Wildershers'** or **'Willocks'**. One of the tribes, the extremely hairy **'Woodwoses'**, are remembered as the hairy-footed Hobbits in Tolkien's books.

The rest of England was referred to as **'The Shires'** and their inhabitants were looked down on as foreigners, or **'furriners'**. In fact, anybody who wasn't born into this elite, South-Eastern corner of England was considered to be a foreigner, until they had been resident for at least twenty five years. If they spoke any language other than Anglo-Saxon or Old English, they were called **'Frenchies'**, irrespective of where they actually came from.

This appellation also applied to the Romano-British and Celtic people who had been pushed back to the mountain fastnesses of Wales in the wake of the Anglo-Saxon invasion. They became referred to as **'Welsh'**, which means 'foreigner' in the old tongue of Britain. Likewise, the word 'walnut' means 'foreign nut', since it had been introduced to our shores by the Romans when they invaded.

The famous British author J.R.R. Tolkien appears to have been another individual with a backbrain full of memories, similar to the Elves. He wove a lot of his folk memories into his stories of Middle-Earth, including 'The Shire' and 'silver-haired Elves' such as Dusty's people.

Returning to the subject of the Downs, it is natural to assume in England that invaders will always come from the South or the South-East, as the Romans and the Normans did, crossing the channel and landing their large expeditionary forces. But there were numerous smaller invasions, by the Anglo-Saxons, the Jutes and other Scandinavians, who approached via the North Sea and descended upon the Weald from the North. After coming ashore and approaching the North Downs from the North, the invaders would climb a long, gentle hill, and would be 500 or 600 feet above sea level before they likely even realised it. The ground would then suddenly have fallen away before them, affording them a magnificent, panoramic view of the rift valley known as the Weald. Perhaps it is this sudden drop after a gentle climb which led to the name of the Downs?

As the all-encompassing ancient forest of England was gradually felled to provide land for farming and living space, little pockets of old woodland still remained dotted across the landscape. The words used to describe these woodlands are still in use today, though most people have forgotten their origins. These descriptive woodland names have often been adopted as surnames among country people.

'**Shaw**' was a name which described a wood hanging onto the side of a steep hill, a bit like a lady's shawl. If it was a very dense wood, with a lot of thick undergrowth, it was called a '**Greenshaw**'. If it contained a lot of stag-headed oaks (some oaks go 'bald' in their old age, with their bare branches resembling a stag's antlers), it was called an '**Oldshaw**'. A shaw full of big trees with little or no undergrowth would be called a '**Bradshaw**'.

Large areas of forested land were still called forests, of course, but when this was taken for use as a surname it was adapted to '**Forrest**'. Smaller forested areas were simply called woods and '**Wood**' is a common surname. When surnames were forced upon the survivors of the Elfin clans in 1742, the '**Chippys**' were one such family group, and they adopted the surname Wood.

The name Wood (much like Miller!) was a good way to disguide an old pagan name in a Christian society. Now anyone who has the surname Wood is prone to get the nickname 'Chippy', even if they don't carry on the woodworking skills of the original Chippy clan who built the Elfin '**Hollow Hill**' homes. Incidentally, there is another meaning hidden in the word '**nickname**' itself. The Devil – and all of the old pagan Deities who were demonised by the Christians – was referred to as 'Old Nick', so a nickname is someone's 'devil name'.

Perhaps this little chapter may help you to view old words with new interest, revealing what bygone treasures may be concealed within them.

wyrdwood: The Story of Dusty Miller

CHAPTER EIGHT

LOOKING AHEAD

We have looked at what Dusty does, and how and why he does it. We have also looked at the distant past and the origins of the Elfin Magick that Dusty uses to help people today. But it is important also for us to look ahead at what the future might bring.

Dusty walks a group around the Woods

Wyrdwood: The Story of Dusty Miller

Why is it so important for us to look to the future and take it into consideration? Well, there are several reasons. For one thing, looking into the future is something Shamen and Witches have always done and been renowned for. Also, it's in our own best interests to be concerned about the future, for reasons that will be discussed below. Not to mention our responsibility to generations yet to come, both Human and Dryad.

A WoodWalk led by Dusty Miller 14th

How does one look to the future? There have been many techniques used over the ages. People today will be used to seeing astrologers and fortune tellers in their daily newspapers. Tarot and tealeaf readers advertise on little cards pinned up in newsagents' windows. In days gone by, soothsayers would look for omens in the flight of birds or other patterns of events.

For those who are especially interested in what methods Dusty might employ to divine the future, there are three within his repertoire that we might consider. He might, of course, choose to read the runes, since he is very skilled in their use and these have long been used for purposes of divination. Those interested can find many fine books on the subject. But Dusty tends to use the runes only in his magical runescripts rather than for forecasting purposes. One technique he certainly uses is simply that of keeping his eyes and his mind open, observing the patterns of events unfolding in the world around him and then extending those patterns, so that he can intuit what is likely to happen. But more than anything else, Dusty will listen to the instructions and the hints of the Folks Upstairs as They communicate with him.

Dusty makes a point during a talk

Wyrdwood: The Story of Dusty Miller

It should be apparent to all readers of this book that Dusty has a set purpose in life, which he is guided to fulfill by the Folks Upstairs. His purpose is to enhance the consciousness of both Human beings and Dryads, bringing a greater understanding between the two, and assisting both species in their spiritual development. As such, it is important that he is able to understand something of what is coming to pass in the world, and he does this through his own keen eye and thoughtfulness, guided by the promptings of his Higher Self, both of which are enhanced by his tricameral brain.

I mentioned earlier that it is important to take thought for the future for our own sakes; that we need to ensure we have a good world to live in. But I didn't only mean that if you are now in your thirties, you will want a decent environment in your seventies. Nor did I mean that you will want to leave a decent world for your children to inhabit. Both of these things are important, of course, but I was referring to something beyond even these. I meant quite literally that you will want to ensure a good future for yourself, beyond your own current lifetime.

Dusty's tribe was from the Indo-European race. So were the Celts and the Germanic tribes who migrated westwards at a much later date. So it is significant that all three of these peoples held the belief that an individual would be reborn into this world sometime after their death, to live a new life. What is more, all three of these peoples held that an individual would generally tend to be reborn within the same clan, tribe or extended family group that they were currently attached to.

I asked Dusty for some clarification of these matters, since some of his comments suggested a belief in reincarnation and also indicated that he had been reborn back into the line of hereditary Elfin Shamen and expected to be so again.

He confirmed that this was the case, and likened the process to a skilled rider bonding with a horse. When the rider needs a new horse, he will tend to return to the same breeder and obtain a horse from the same stock, so that he will enjoy a similar experience and relationship with his new steed. It is a question of slipping into a pair of comfortable shoes that have been 'worn in' and properly adjusted to fit. The soul tends to seek out the same genetic template for its next incarnation.

With his well developed FamilyMemory, Dusty has a good knowledge of his prior lives. He indicated that he is also given knowledge of when he will next be 'on duty', when his next life as hereditary Shaman will begin. However, he is not told when his current life will end, not exactly; that has to come as a surprise.

Dusty Miller 14th

Wyrdwood: The Story of Dusty Miller

Dusty then went on to say that in between these main 'tours of duty', the spirit may take holidays, living more restful lives or trying out new things. He explained that between his last lifetime as a Shaman and his current one, he experienced two other 'holiday' lives. In the first of these he was a woman in India, a servant who did the cooking in a household. He recalls a visitor to the house, someone he was afraid of. This was a large woman who smelled like a man and smoked cigars. It was only when reading *The Secret Doctrine* during his current life that he realised that this fearsome woman was the legendary H.P. Blavatsky. His next life was a shorter one, spent in China, and when Dusty was born into his current incarnation, he was still able to paint in the Chinese style until he entered his teens and the remembered ability finally left him.

So one very good reason for taking thought for the future and the state of the world around us is that we are going to have to live in it, long after the death of our current selves. So that may provide an environmental incentive to even the most selfish or lackadaisical.

Anyone worth their salt will be equally concerned for the future of others, of course, and Dusty's entire work is directed towards helping people. It is probably apparent to all that the world around us is changing and that we need to be prepared to adapt to those changes and to help those disadvantaged by them to get back on their feet.

The world is shifting politically and economically and these are factors that the people who live on the planet need to use their voice in if changes are to be for the benefit of all instead of just a few. The world is also undergoing natural changes, as it always has done. The climate is shifting and the poles are shifting. The Earth's magnetic poles are known to have flipped several times in the past. Who can tell what effects this change in magnetic fields would have upon the technology-led civilisation we have today, should it happen again? For there are many scientists who argue from the records that such a shift is once again due. All the evidence seems to point to fairly dramatic changes over the next few years. And where changes occur dramatically, there are always going to be people who suffer as a result of them.

So as we look to the future, our imperative is to be in the right place at the right time to be able to help people. By keeping our eyes open and thinking upon facts rather than theories, observing what is actually happening in the world around us, we may be able to do just that.

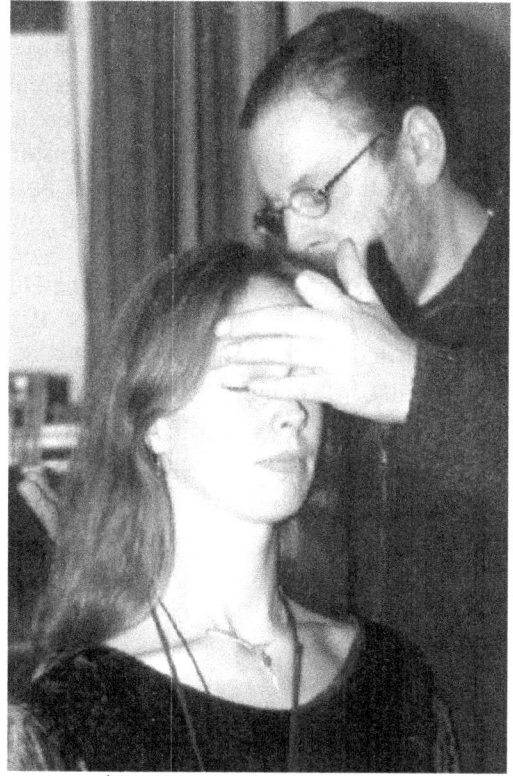

Dusty 14th using LiveWood to give a Blessing

Wyrdwood: The Story of Dusty Miller

The other important task is to expand the network of Humans and Dryads working together to create a better future. Dusty has devoted his life's work to this task, creating LiveWood tools in quantities that would have been undreamed of at any time in the past, all ready to be picked up and used by the person they resonate most strongly with. He has brought the worlds of Humans and Dryads closer together than they have been at any time since his ancestors lived in the forest prior to the arrival of the Celts on these shores. His son, Dusty 14th, now continues that work just as passionately, giving talks internationally and introducing ever increasing numbers of people to the wonders of LiveWood and Dryad consciousness.

I hope that this account of Dusty's work with the Dryads has been of interest and has opened a few minds to the world around us, inhabited by intelligences different from our own, a fact which was well known by our ancestors but has been forgotten amid the artificiality of modern living, which often distances us from nature (including our own human nature).

If you would like to know more about the Dustys, or if you would like to acquire a LiveWood artifact of your own, visit the website listed in the 'Further Reading' section and follow the links there. Speaking personally, I now have three LiveWood items and am becoming firm friends with my Dryad companions, who are making life much easier in many respects. I hope that readers of this book may feel moved to make a similar connection themselves.

Wyrdwood: The Story of Dusty Miller

GLOSSARY

Throughout this book, certain words have been used with spellings slightly different to the usual, or in unusual ways. This is because Dusty has developed a vocabulary for the work he does and the invisible, higher world with which he deals. So he will occasionally spell a word differently, or use it in an unusual way, to signify that he is using the word to refer to a concept beyond the ordinary. Dusty always tries to make his language as plain and untechnical as possible, but he has compiled the following glossary of 'Elfinspeak' so that readers might understand the precise way in which he uses words and what exactly he means by them.

Apologies if anything remains obscure or unclear; this is the best possible attempt to explain the meanings behind these words, but it can be difficult to translate right-brain concepts into left-brain worded explanations.

LeftBrain -

This is the Left Hemisphere of that part of the human brain that is called the Cerebral Cortex. It is very Sola orientated and tends to be scientific and analytical in its approach to life; it likes to understand what is going on and reason things out for itself. It thinks in a sequential and linear fashion. It also tends to be dominated by words, figures and symbols, and appears to be unable to accept information put to it in any other form. It is liable, therefore, to suffer from all manner of inhibitions and mental blocks of its own making.

This is unfortunate, as its reasoning ability is by far the most developed on this planet. Although its potential for thinking is to all intentions limitless, for some reason unknown to me it seems to spend a lot of its time just accepting what it considers to be facts, and not actually doing any thinking for itself. If a fact is presented to it that doesn't fit in with its preconceived ideas, it will on most occasions reject it out of hand, without even examining it.

RightBrain -

This is the Right Hemisphere of the Cerebral Cortex, and is very Luna orientated. It's excellent at lateral thinking and making quantum leaps in its quest for knowledge. As all its experiences appear to be recorded in the form of three dimensional pictures (in full technicolour), augmented with the full gamut of feelings and emotions, it is quite capable of making valid decisions on an intuitive basis, without any apparent logic (much to the annoyance of the LeftBrain).

Although this hemisphere of the brain is very creative, as well as artistic, it requires some careful handling, and most people never get around to learning how to put it to good use. The funny thing about this situation is the fact that those who do try to use their RightBrain are often held up to ridicule by those who can't be bothered to even try. If you care to stop and think for a moment, you'll probably find that right now your LeftBrain and RightBrain are busy contradicting each other as to the meaning of these words.

There's no doubt about it, these new brains (the Cerebral Cortex) are really marvellous, but we need to make a lot more effort towards increasing their effectiveness and compatibility. Maybe in the forthcoming Aquarian Age, we'll leave the left-hand path of logic and explore the right-hand path of intuition.

OldBrain -
That part of the human brain that is known today as the Cerebellum. This is the remnant of the old bicameral brain, that most people stopped using once the Cerebral Cortex, with its multipurpose right and left hemispheres, had been developed. It is where our family memory bank appears to be centred and is Jaia orientated, which enables it to Know Things and Cause Coincidences without any LeftBrain or RightBrain activity. It also has the ability to act as an Auto-Pilot whenever we need one, and appears to be in control of all the body's automotive reflex actions, such as breathing, locomotion, and scratching to relieve an itch.

FamilyMemory -
This is our term for the tribal memory bank, that the inheritors of the wisdom in Dusty's family learn to tap into during their Shamanic apprenticeship. It appears to be somewhat similar to the Akashic Memory in eastern philosophy, and consists of countless pictures of everyday life, stretching back into the prehistoric past.

You know how something simple, like the smell of new mown hay, can be very evocative, and conjure up picture memories from your childhood? Well, our FamilyMemory is very much like that. Dusty cannot call it up just by saying, "What happened on such and such a date?", as it just doesn't seem to work that way. But on many, many occasions somebody will ask him a question, and he will automatically answer them from his own remembered experience; and then later, he'll suddenly realise that that particular experience didn't happen to him in this current body, but was accessed from the recorded memory of either one of his ancestors, or one of his own previous incarnations, and probably occurred many centuries ago.

I suppose you could call it a sort of intuitive knowing that not only surpasses understanding, but is very reliable. It certainly enriches Dusty's enjoyment of life, but of course, he's used to it; it's the people who ask him the questions who often find his multi-level memory and OldBrain answers somewhat confusing.

Sola or MyLord -

This is the Elves' name for the Sun and the God who guides our Higher Self and takes a personal interest in our welfare. He is the tutor who is responsible for developing and teaching us how to use our LeftBrain. Has a tendency to think that His method is the only method and His brain the only one we should use. Is very insistent on the use of words and definitions as an aid to understanding. It was He who insisted that we included this glossary. He is also the original, external, and jealous God, so I'm being very careful what I say.

Luna or MyLady -

This is the Elves' name for the Moon and the Goddess who guides our Higher Self and takes a great personal interest in both our well-being and welfare. She is the tutor responsible for the development and training of our RightBrain. She uses a discovery method of teaching, utilising multicoloured pictures, sensations, feelings and emotions, to help you to know what you need to know. 'Belief' is not a requisite in Her method of teaching, you either Know or you don't Know, (i.e. Intuitive Knowledge).

Wyrdwood: The Story of Dusty Miller

Jaia or GranMother -

The Elves' name for the supreme feminine life-force, which to them is the Earth (planet) on which we stand. She is also Mother Nature, and She who was and still is, Mother of us all. On the other hand, She is the Wise Goddess, who is always available (via our OldBrain) when we need guidance. Please Note: The Elves show Her their love and the respect they have for her, by spelling her name with a soft 'J' instead of a hard 'G' like the other tribes do.

Aether or GranFather -

Pronounced Ether, this is the Elves' name for the supreme masculine life-force which they feel is represented by the sky, the very air we breathe, and in fact the whole atmosphere that surrounds the planet Earth, as He holds Her in His arms. He is a strange, silent God, who doesn't appear to show much interest in us, as He seems to have other problems on His mind. He does, however, keep a blueprint of each of us, and should He at any time turn his back on us, we'd all be dead within minutes. Although, like a benevolent grandfather, He supplies us with a virtually unlimited supply of energy, He can be a bit violent when provoked.

The WildWood -

When the Elves first came here, this land was clothed in natural, broad-leaf woodland, which suited both them and the wild pigs they hunted for food. To them it was a land of plenty, so they settled here and Dusty's family have been here ever since. As their FamilyMemory appears to date from this period, they've always referred to it as the 'Days of the WildWood', but historians call it the New Stone Age.

Wyrdwood: The Story of Dusty Miller

Sacred Trees -
All the Trees that grew wild in Western Europe, in the part that we now know as 'The British Isles', before mankind first arrived there, are in the Elfin opinion 'Sacred Trees'. They grew there because they wanted to grow there, they were not planted by man. The primordial forest in which Dusty does his work is full of wild Trees that have been living and constantly re-generating there for well over 50,000 years. They were extremely ancient when his remote ancestors set up home there some 40,000 years ago, and have been continuing to re-generate there ever since.

In Dusty's part of England, they were not flattened by the glaciers of the Ice Age, and survived as a very dense forest until the Celts started to clear them to make farmland. Luckily for the Elves, some of their hillsides were too steep for farming and so a few strips of this incredibly ancient forest still survive to this day.

The Celts, and all the other invaders since them, have introduced all sorts of new Trees to the landscape, but the Elves don't consider them to be Sacred. Since then, gardeners and now scientists have spent a lot of time and energy, hybridization, to produce 'better trees' with bigger, tastier fruit, etc. But unfortunately this has resulted in a great loss of intelligence. In equivalent human terms, you would call these 'new, improved trees' very 'institutionalised', as they just do not have any of the 'streetwise' survival instinct and high intelligence of their wild cousins. Which is why the Elves only work with Wild Sacred Trees.

Tree Dryads -
Every living Tree shares a 'Higher Self' with the other Trees in its tribal group. This higher self is similar to our higher self, soul or spirit (call it what you will) and is normally termed as a Tree Spirit. Human words like 'Tree Spirit' don't mean much to real Tree Spirits as they haven't any ears to hear

Wyrdwood: The Story of Dusty Miller

them with, so they don't take much notice. However, if you use the ancient Aegean word 'Dryad', your thoughts as you say the word produce a series of mental synapses that in turn trigger off a series of brainwaves that they can pick up in some way. We don't know just how this works, but the effects are very noticeable, for you suddenly find every Tree Spirit in the vicinity looking at you and taking interest. A very sobering effect indeed.

TreeTribes -

This is the Elfin term for the many types of trees that exist, such as Hazel, Yew, Beech, Rowan, etc., etc. Each tribe has its own individual characteristics, which give its members a corporate identity, as well as a distinctive vibration, as a means of recognition to us mere mortals. For further details, see any good book on Trees and their identification, but remember they will call them species and sub-species, not TreeTribes.

Wands and Cudgels -

Both of these are LiveWood items that Dusty's family has been producing for countless centuries.

A Wand is a short stick or baton, made of LiveWood, that can be used in the right hands to produce, direct or receive energy of the psychic levels. Healers and Shamen use them to 'Channel' Healing Energy and direct it into their patient, whereas Witches use them to make things happen in accordance with their will. However, there are so many other uses that it would take all day to list them here.

In the old days they were often used as a badge of office or to show authority, but nowadays this type are usually called Sceptres. A Bishop's Crosier is a fine example of a Shepherd's Crook being used as a mark of authority.

In the olden days, these were often shown in pictures, stained-glass windows and sculptures as having at least one or two leaves attached. This was to show that they were made of LiveWood. A good example of this can be seen in the Rider-Wait Tarot Pack.

There are many pictures of wands in this book that will give you an idea of what is available, but please bear in mind the two Dustys have a repertoire of over three hundred wands that they could make, and that every one they produce is a unique individual, as they never achieve the same shape twice.

Cudgels on the other hand are a form of Walking-stick with a heavy handle, that can be used for defence. In the UK we have three basic sorts of sticks for walking with, each with its own sort of craftsman to make them. We have Walking-stick Makers who bend sticks to the right shape; Stick-Dressers who add handles carved from wood, bone, horn or antler to straightened sticks and Cudgel Craftsmen who make all sizes of stick from natural branches, without any artificial bends or joints.

As the last surviving 'LiveWood' Cudgel Craftsmen in the world, the two Dustys fall into the last category.

For further information on all the Wands and other LiveWood products on offer, see the Dustys' LiveWood Site, whose link can be found in the 'Further Reading' section following this Glossary.

LeyLines -
The whole surface of our planet (Jaia) appears to be criss-crossed with energy lines, similar to the acupuncture meridians on the human body. These lines are now known as Leys or Leylines, but Dusty's FamilyMemory refers to them as Powerlines, because they were such an excellent energy source for magical work (Earth Magic, etc).

Leylines are a very interesting subject, but rather too

big to tackle here, so I would recommend that you read some of the excellent books on them, written by such people as Watkins, Graves, Screeton, Devereux, etc.

LeyCross -
    Wherever two or more Leylines cross over each other, their energy flows cause a reciprocal power vortex to be formed. We think of these as being equivalent to Jaia's Pulse, and treat them with great respect. The more Leylines involved in the cross-over, the more powerful the vortex.

    Personally, the Dustys live and work in a multi-LeyCross, and can assure you that it really hums. For some unknown reason, the veil between the worlds is much thinner on Leylines, enabling contact to be made. This is even more so, in a Ley Vortex; for they always seem to contain a portal to the other worlds that parallel this one.

ShaMen -
    The member of the tribe responsible for all magical operations and contacts with the other worlds. Also acts as the translator of information from the deities to the tribe and helps the individual tribe members to develop their RightBrain and LeftBrain abilities. This is normally an inherited task, utilising information and skills passed down from generation to generation, plus access to a FamilyMemory.

    There is a saying that it doesn't matter if a Shaman is a man, or a woman, or both, as long as they can ride the Sha! The 'Shaa' is a name for the principle energy used (which is akin to Chi, Ki, Prana, etc), and is very powerful.

The British Aboriginals -
    In the Days of the WildWood, before this land became

an island, there were, to the best of Dusty's knowledge, three aboriginal races living here. They were quiet, peaceful folk, living in small tribes. They had bicameral or group minds, with a non-verbal communication system that suited their way of life. Having a fully functioning OldBrain, they were not only in constant contact with all the tribe, but also their ancestors and the Deities.

It was about that time that something akin to the hundredth monkey syndrome occurred, and people all over the world started to develop a new type of brain (the Cerebral Cortex). They were still developing their skill at using their marvellous RightBrain and LeftBrain in a balanced sort of manner when they were invaded and subjugated by the LeftBrain dominated Boat People.

Each aboriginal race had its own characteristics, (see below) but the absence of 'half-moons' on the fingers and toes was common to them all. Later their descendants were to boast that they were so Luna orientated, that they didn't need the half-moons to remind them of their duties.

The Elfin Folk -

The aboriginal stock from which Dusty's family is descended. Although of average height, they were inclined to be shorter than the Celtic peoples and so they got called the little people. They had pink skin with reddish hair, turning silver in maturity. They also had very little body hair, but a profusion of freckles. Their tribe were Tree Elves, and lived in the woods with their totem animal the wild pig. The Dusty Family were the Hereditary Shamen to the Saelig Silvadobbs, as their particular tribe of Tree Elves were known.

The Horned Ones -

The tallest of the aboriginal races in this country. Not

only were they taller than the Elves, they were much bigger boned, strong and brawny, like their totem animal, the Auroch (the forerunner of what we now call Kine or Cattle). They had dark, swarthy skin, with long, black hair, a lot of thick, curly body-hair and really shaggy eyebrows. It was the latter that gave rise to the Elves' name for them, for they used to wax their eyebrows into horns like their cattle, in the same way as the Elves waxed their moustaches into tusks. They used to decorate and enhance their sacred places with the huge stones that are now referred to as Megaliths.

The Hairy Ones -
    The third and probably oldest of the races that originally occupied this land, having walked here long before the English Channel cut us off from the continent. Unlike the ectomorphic Elves and the mesomorphic Horned Folk, the Hairy Folk were very definitely endomorphs: short, plump, fleshy and almost completely covered in a tawny mass of curly body hair. They didn't, however, look like Wolf-Man, for their hair was in fact like a soft down, that enhanced their appearance, and combined with their ready smile and friendly disposition, gave them a teddybear-like appeal to all who met them.
    Unlike the Elves, they were excellent swimmers and really loved the ice-cold water in the British streams and rivers, which is probably why they had taken the humble Otter as their totem animal.
    Another not usually seen but very distinctive feature about them, was the fact that they had a little rudimentary tail about two inches long. It is interesting to note that although they died out as a separate race in the Dark Ages (they were then known as Woodwoses), their genes must have carried on in their intermarried descendants, for a group of English soldiers captured in the Napoleonic wars had tails, and gave

rise to the French propaganda that all Englishmen were devils.

The Dwarves -
These were the first people to invade the woodlands, after Britain became cut off from the continent by the newly formed English Channel. Unfortunately for the aboriginals, they were into metalworking and with their bronze swords they introduced aggression and bloodshed to this land; and suddenly the halcyon days of the 'Golden Age' were over.

They were short, dark haired and muscular, with a very aggressive bearing and truculent look, that the Elves found very disturbing. For the first time, they learned to fear strangers, and as a result they kept out of their way as much as possible.

The Boat People -
This is the Elves' name for the hoards of iron-sword bearing people, who were the next invaders to arrive here. Nowadays, they are referred to collectively as The Celts, (or Kelts, depending upon your romantic leanings). In fact, they were many tribes, who arrived here by way of the sea over several centuries; riding inland on their large horses, taking whatever they wanted until they occupied the whole country.

From then on the Elves became not only a minority race, but a fugitive one as well, given the derogatory name 'Færiefolc' (Fairyfolk) by their new overlords. So now they had to become experts at camouflage and cunning in order to survive, and that was the start of the fade-into-the-background existence that the Elves have lived ever since.

The Boat People brought many new ideas and attitudes to this land that were to have all sorts of long term effects on the future generations of British Islanders.

Although they arrived here in waves, spread over a

long period of time, they all spoke the same language, so they must have had a common origin. Their language skill amazed the Elves: so many words yet so few gestures; their pictures were stylised and came second place to nouns and adjectives. They seemed to give a name to anything and everything, so that they didn't need to observe it any more, just remember its name. And what is more they never seemed to stop talking, which probably explains why they had lost contact with their OldBrain. They were very Sola orientated, for their LeftBrain was obviously the dominant one, with the other two being ignored almost completely.

Being a hybrid race themselves, they were the first to bring the idea of racial intermixture to this land, and now we're a whole country of mixed racial stock. This, of course, isn't such a bad thing, as it tends to level out the extremes in social behaviour, inherent in pure but inbred racial stock.

It is also interesting to note that we all carry genes that give physiological throwback indications from many of our various remote ancestors. Such as moonless fingernails, tufted eyebrows, or ears that are lobeless, hairy, or both.

Another thing the Boat People introduced, was bright and beautiful clothing and jewelry; so different from the functional, melt-into-the-background outfits the Elves wore.

Mind you, Dusty relates that the Elves were rather shocked by the Celts' love of undressing in public, and especially the way they used to strip off naked to fight. It's very intimidating to be attacked by hoards of naked warriors waving their weapons.

They were excellent jewelers and metal workers, and introduced the Elves to all sorts of new tools, designs, machines and structures to improve the quality of life. Looking back on them now, Dusty would say that although they were barbaric in some ways they were very civilised in others, and all in all the Elves learnt a lot from them. If nothing else, they certainly forced the tribes, albeit indirectly, to develop and use their Left- and RightBrains effectively, for their very survival depended upon it.

The Xians -
This is a sort of blanket word to cover all those solar orientated, patriarchal, religious sects, who call themselves Christians, because their beliefs are loosely based on the teachings of Jesus of Nazareth.

Unfortunately, these sects tend to be very intolerant of each other, and very bigoted in their attitude to all other religious groups; which makes them very difficult to converse with, especially as they are the current overlords of Albion's Isles of the Blessed.

Still, that's their affair; 'Live and let live' should be our motto. After all, what right have we to tell them how they should worship their God; what is right for them is right for them, and nothing to do with us. May they, like us, be blessed by being always in the eyes of the Divine!

The MillerClan -
These are a group of very dedicated LiveWood Users, who are actively helping the Dustys to promote Dryad Consciousness through their Elfin Art. Although not blood relatives to the Dusty line, they all have an Elfin connection, so the Dustys treat them like members of the family.

LiveWood User -
Anybody who has built-up a partnership with a Tame Dryad (i.e. a Dryad resident within a piece of LiveWood) in order to improve their personal abilities and develop their Dryad Consciousness, and thereby be of greater service to both Mankind and Dryadkind as they progress along their own

particular path to perfection.

Magick -
    To Dusty, Magick is something that works on many levels of consciousness to produce results. Although the effects may be unaccountable and often baffling to people whose idea of reality is limited to the so-called physical world, they are, nevertheless, completely natural to anyone with an expanded consciousness.
    Dusty does, however, spell it in the old fashioned way, with a final 'k' to show that it is rather different to the 'Magic Tricks' of the Stage Magician.
    If you think of your 'Mind' as being somewhat similar to a computer, then Dusty's Magick and especially his 'Magic Spells' or 'Thought-forms' are specially written software programs to enable it do all sorts of useful things that will benefit your Mind, your Body, and your Spirit, all at the same time.

MoonSymbols -
    These are the symbols, (illustrated in chapter six) that were used for countless centuries, by Shamen who couldn't read and write, to identify the various Luna Months. Over the years they've become somewhat stylised, but at least they're easily recognisable, and quite decorative.

Runes -
    This is an ancient Germanic alphabet that can be used to produce magickal results. There seem to be as many versions as there were Germanic Tribes, and there are now many books on the subject, each claiming to have the official version. Dusty has a version that was stolen from King

wyrdwood: The Story of Dusty Miller

Hengist of Kent towards the end of the 5th century, some two generations before the time of King Arthur.

As the Elves were unable to read or write, they just considered them a very useful group of Magickal Signs that they could use; not an alphabet. In fact, they got so interested in their Magickal use that they started to collect any other Rune they came across, with the result that Dusty now has an alphabet of thirty-five Runes, each with a secret meaning that he is not at liberty to divulge for safety reasons.

If you are interested in Runes, then Dusty would advise you to read some of the books available on the subject, and be careful to 'read between the lines'. If you are meant to understand and use them, you intuition will guide you to success without harmful side-effects.

"Blessed Be!" -

This is a very old Elfin phrase that has been passed down through the ages as a reminder of their sacred inheritance. Back in the Days of the WildWood (now known as the New Stone Age), the Elves knew that wherever they went and whatever they did, they were always within the eyesight of their Divinities, (now referred to as The Gods before The Gods); and they acted accordingly.

Even the Celts who called them the Filthy People (Faeriefolc — Fairy Folk), because they had soap and the Elves didn't, noticed that they were in their eyes, 'touched by the Gods', and referred to their holy innocence as being 'Blessed' (Saelig).

Throughout the many centuries since Britain was first invaded by the Celts, the Elves were treated as sub-humans, and so they boosted their morale by repeating "Saelig Sie!" to one another, to remind themselves that the Old Gods were still on their side. Over the years, with the development of the Old English language, it became "Blessed Be!", and then during the persecution times it was reduced to "Be Be!", and it still lingers on in modern English as "Bye Bye!".

Unfortunately, nowadays 'Saelig' has been reduced to 'Silly' and 'Blessed' to 'Good'; but the Elfin Folk still use it in the old context. After all, although they got the Bill of Rights in 1951, they are not 'out of the wood' yet. For as far as discrimination is concerned, they still have to tread softly, as any member of a 'minority group' knows.

However, things are changing very quickly these days and getting better all the time. So the Dustys say to you, recognise the holiness within yourself, so that you too may be like them and be blessed, by being always in the eyes of the Divine!

Wyrdwood: The Story of Dusty Miller

Wyrdwood: The Story of Dusty Miller

FURTHER READING

T.C. Lethbridge, Tom Graves and Janet Hoult, *The Essential T.C. Lethbridge*, published by Routledge and Kegan Paul, 1980.

T.C. Lethbridge, *The Power of the Pendulum*, published by Arkana, 1989.

Terry Pratchett, *The Wee Free Men*, published by Corgi Childrens, 2004.

Terry Pratchett, *A Hat Full of Sky*, published by Corgi Childrens, 2005.

Terry Pratchett, *Wintersmith*, published by Corgi Childrens, 2007.

Terry Pratchett, *I Shall Wear Midnight*, published by Doubleday Childrens, 2010.

Terry Pratchett, *Johnny and the Bomb*, published by Corgi Childrens, 2004.

Alfred Watkins, *The Old Straight Track*, published by Abacus, 1994.

Wyrdwood: The Story of Dusty Miller

DVD

"I'm an Elf", **Dusty Miller 13**[th] **Talk Antropia 2006**, published by Open Eye Productions, Diemen, The Netherlands, 2009. Now available in the UK. Contact: **dusty@dusty13.tk**

Essential Web Sites

Dusty Miller 13th **on Twitter (New and Up to Date):**
http://twitter.com/dusty13th

The LiveWood Site of Dusty Miller 13th**:**
http://www.livewood.nl/

LiveWood Arts and Crafts by Dusty 14th **and Claudia Miller:**
http://www.lebensholz.org/

Dusty Miller 14th's and Claudia's LiveWood Pages:
http://livewood-lebensholz.weebly.com/

Site to Obtain and Print Your Charged Copy of the Runescript to Keep You Safe:
http://www.dustys-lebensholz.de/RuneScript.html

The Tricameral Mind:
http://www.qondio.com/the-tricameral-mind

Introducing the Dustys:
http://www.bostochten.nl/dusty/lws/index.php?page=dusties.htm

An Account of a Walk With Dusty:
http://tinkerbell-nl.blogspot.com/2006/04/dusty-miller.html

Dusty Miller 13th's MySpace Page:
http://www.myspace.com/dusty13th

Dusty Miller 13th's Blog on MySpace:
http://www.myspace.com/dusty13th/blog

Dusty Miller 13th's Youtube Channel:
http://www.youtube.com/profile?gl=GB&hl=en-GB&user=dusty13th

Dusty's Blog of 'Curious Ideas That Can Help You Get Ahead':
http://www.curious-ideas.blogspot.com/

German Language Websites

http://www.dustys-lebensholz.de/
http://www.dustys-lebensholz.de/Mailorder.html
http://livewood-lebensholz.weebly.com/dates-2011---termine-2011.html
http://livewood-lebensholz.weebly.com/index.html
http://www.lebensholz.org/services

SERVICES

Public Talks and Seminars

Both the Dusties are available to give Talks and Seminars, both at home and abroad.
    Instructional Field Trips to Ancient (3,000 or 4,000 year old) Trees, Lectures at Exhibitions, even Interviews on Radio and Television, anything considered.
    The Dusties may be contacted with a view to arranging Talks at the following email address:

dusty@dusty13.tk

LiveWood by Mail Order

If you wish to obtain a LiveWood tool or pendant for your own use by mail order, visit the following website:

http://millerclan.tk

or send an email to the following address:

dusty@dusty13.tk

Wyrdwood: The Story of Dusty Miller

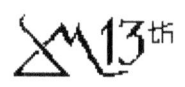

Wyrdwood: The Story of Dusty Miller